THE UN\

NOTES

including
- *Life and Background*
- *Yoknapatawpha County: The Sartorises and*
   the Snopeses
- *List of Characters*
- *Sartoris Genealogy*
- *Critical Commentaries:*
   Ambuscade
   Retreat
   Raid
   Riposte in Tertio
   Vendée
   Skirmish at Sartoris
   An Odor of Verbena
- *Character Analyses*
- *Questions for Review*
- *Selected Bibliography*

by
James L. Roberts, Ph.D.
Department of English
University of Nebraska

INCORPORATED
LINCOLN, NEBRASKA 68501

Editor

Gary Carey, M.A.
University of Colorado

Consulting Editor

James L. Roberts, Ph.D.
Department of English
University of Nebraska

ISBN 0-8220-1316-9
© Copyright 1980
by
C. K. Hillegass
All Rights Reserved
Printed in U.S.A.

1991 Printing

Cliffs Notes, Inc.   Lincoln, Nebraska

CONTENTS

THE UNVANQUISHED NOTES

LIFE AND BACKGROUND

The Unvanquished is the novel that is most often recommended as an introduction to Faulkner's fiction. It is, in one sense, his easiest novel to read, and it presents many of the characters and ideas that are found in his other greater novels. Furthermore, the novel is based in large part on Faulkner's own great-grandfather's exploits, and it presents both a romantic view of the South, and it shows the flaws in the southern culture which caused its downfall. Faulkner shows "the old order" of the South fighting for survival and, ultimately, failing. Most of the characters in the novel think that the southern way of life is the "right" way of life, the best way of life—in short, a way of life in accordance with divine law. In Miss Rosa Millard's prayer to God, she says, "now that You have seen to make our cause a lost cause," indicating that she still believes the ways of the South are right; she question's Gods purpose, but she cannot deny God.

William Faulkner was born in New Albany, Mississippi, on September 25, 1897, but his family soon moved to Oxford, Mississippi. Almost all of his novels take place in and around Oxford, which he renamed Jefferson, Mississippi. Even though Faulkner is a contemporary American writer, he is already considered to be one of the world's greatest writers. In 1949, he was awarded the Nobel Prize for Literature, the highest literary prize that can be awarded to a writer. When he accepted this prize, he maintained that the duty of the artist was to depict the human heart in conflict with itself. This attitude is best realized in the final story of this collection, "An Odor of Verbena," when Bayard Sartoris must decide what course of action he must take to avenge his father's murder.

Faulkner came from an old, proud, and distinguished Mississippi family, which included a governor, a colonel in the Confederate Army, and notable business pioneers. His great-grandfather, Colonel William Culbert Falkner (the "u" was added to Faulkner's name by mistake when his first novel was published, and Faulkner retained the misspelling), came to Mississippi from South Carolina during the first part of the nineteenth century. The Colonel appears in many of Faulkner's novels under the name of Colonel John Sartoris. Colonel William Falkner had a rather distinguished career as a soldier both in the Mexican War and in the Civil War. During the Civil War, Falkner's hot temper caused him to be demoted from full Colonel to Lieutenant Colonel. After the war, Falkner was heavily involved in the trials of the Reconstruction period. He killed several men during this time and became a rather notorious figure. He also joined in with a partner and built the first railroad during Reconstruction; then he quarrelled with his partner, and the partnership broke up. When his former partner ran for the state legislature, Colonel Falkner ran against him and soundly defeated him. Thus, as one can easily see, the character of Colonel Sartoris in *The Unvanquished* is based rather heavily upon the career of Faulkner's own great-grandfather. This could account for some of the ambivalent characterization associated with Colonel Sartoris.

Faulkner was once asked at the University of Virginia, where he was a guest lecturer, how much he drew his characterization of Colonel Sartoris from his own great-grandfather, Colonel Falkner. Faulkner responded:

> That's difficult to say. That comes back to what we spoke of—the three sources the writer draws from—and I myself would have to stop and go page by page to see just how much I drew from family annals that I had listened to from these old undefeated spinster aunts that children of my time grew up with. Probably, well, the similarity of raising of that infantry regiment, that was the same, the—his death was about—was pretty close, pretty close parallel, but the rest of it I would have go through to—page by page and remember, Did I hear this or did I imagine this?

What does not appear in the novel is that during all of these involved activities, Colonel Falkner took out time to write one of the nation's best sellers, *The White Rose of Memphis*, which appeared in 1880. He also wrote two other novels, but only his first was an outstanding success. As was Colonel Sartoris in *The Unvanquished*, Colonel Falkner was finally killed by one of his rivals, and his death was never avenged. Today, one can travel to the cemetery in Oxford,

Mississippi, and see a statue of Colonel Falkner, dressed in his Confederate uniform, gazing out at his railroad, and looking over the region that he fought so desperately and valiantly for. Only William Faulkner himself, of all the interceding members of the Falkner family, was as distinguished—and ultimately more distinguished—than his great-grandfather was.

Except for his novel *Sanctuary*, Faulkner's early novels were never commercial successes. Consequently, he would often interrupt a novel and write short stories for magazines; most of the stories in *The Unvanquished*, for example, first appeared in magazines. He would also take frequent trips to Hollywood, where he wrote or collaborated in writing film scripts purely for financial reasons. When *Intruder in the Dust* was published in 1948 and was almost immediately made into a movie, the novel and the movie both called attention to all of Faulkner's other works. Almost overnight, Faulkner was acclaimed by all sorts of critics, writers, and teachers. Ironically, virtually all of his books were out of print at that time, but today one can readily purchase a copy of almost every book that Faulkner ever wrote.

In his later life, in 1955, Faulkner moved to Virginia, where he was artist-in-residence at the University of Virginia; there, in informal class settings, he answered many questions about his books, his writing, and his artistic concepts. While he was not always accurate, his answers to many of the questions are expansions on his entire Yoknapatawpha series. Of *The Unvanquished*, he said that it should be the first of his novels that one should read because "it's easy to read. Compared to the others, I mean. . . ." When asked if he had written the stories with the idea in mind that they would someday become a novel, Faulkner responded:

> I saw them as a long series. I had never thought of it in terms of a novel, exactly. I realized that they would be too episodic to be what I considered a novel, so I thought of them as a series of stories . . . when I got into the first one I could see two more, but by the time I'd finished the first one I saw that it was going further than that, and then when I'd finished the fourth one, I had postulated too many questions that I had to answer for my own satisfaction. So the others had to be . . . written then.

In all of his work, Faulkner used new techniques to express his views of man's position in the modern world. In his early works, Faulkner viewed with despair man's position in the universe. He saw man as a weak creature incapable of rising above his selfish needs. Later Faulkner's view changed. In his more recent works, it is clear that he believed man to be potentially great, or, in the words of Faulkner's Nobel Prize acceptance speech, man shall "not only endure; he will prevail." In almost all of his novels, Faulkner penetrated deeply into the psychological motivations for man's actions and investigated man's dilemma in the modern world.

YOKNAPATAWPHA COUNTY: THE SARTORISES AND THE SNOPESES

Faulkner created the mythological county of Yoknapatawpha in his third novel, *Flags in the Dust*. This particular novel, however, was not published during Faulkner's lifetime; it appeared posthumously in 1973. As a result, Faulkner's readers were introduced to Yoknapatawpha County in *Sartoris* (1929), a heavily edited and much shorter version of *Flags in the Dust*. The name "Yoknapatawpha" is a word Faulkner devised by combining the Indian words for the two rivers, the Yokna and the Patawpha, which form the southern border of this county. Faulkner called the county seat Jefferson and, later, he drew a map of the county (which can be found in all editions of his novel *Absalom, Absalom!* 1936), showing where many events in the various novels take place.

In *Flags in the Dust*, Faulkner deals with later generations of the Sartoris family (the central family of *The Unvanquished*, 1938). Bayard Sartoris is an old man, Aunt Jenny Du Pre still looks after the Sartoris mansion, and some of the black servants (Joby, Louvinia, and Simon) are still employed. In fact, even though Colonel Sartoris has been dead for over forty years, Simon still talks to him about the changing times.

One of the greatnesses of Faulkner's mythological county that many of the same characters are found in many of the different novels; a character who appears in a minor role in one novel might later be a significant character in another novel. Many of his characters, thus, appear in numerous novels in varying roles, and, therefore, in reading more than one of Faulkner's novels, we come to know a great deal about all of the various people who live in

Yoknapatawpha County. For example, after having read about Granny (Miss Rosa) and having come to feel that we actually know her in *The Unvanquished*, we are then prepared for certain types of actions or reactions from her in a short story published many years later, entitled "My Grandmother Millard and General Bedford Forrest and the Battle of Harrykin Creek." In fact, this story has only a few characters in it that are not found in *The Unvanquished*.

In *Flags in the Dust*, the presence of Colonel Sartoris still pervades the entire countryside. His memory is constantly evoked by various characters in the novel, and his deeds and exploits are still recounted. Likewise, some of the old Negroes are still with the Sartoris family. Louvinia, who in "Retreat" helped Colonel Sartoris escape from the Yankees by holding his boots and pistols for him, is still working for the Sartorises in 1919. Likewise, Joby, her husband, is still there. And, as was noted, even though Colonel Sartoris has been dead for over forty years, Simon still talks to him and complains about how things are changing.

In addition to Simon's reminiscing about Colonel Sartoris, other characters evoke memories of him. Aunt Jenny Du Pre also likes to narrate past episodes of the Sartoris family, especially some of the antics of Colonel John Sartoris and his brother, Bayard I. For example, she delights in telling about a raid on a Yankee camp which Bayard I led, stealing most of their provisions and capturing a Yankee colonel, who casually mentioned that at least Bayard I did not capture the anchovies. Upon hearing this, Bayard I foolishly charged back into the camp and was killed in an attempt to capture the anchovies. This type of foolhardy bravado in the midst of a serious war characterizes the actions of many of the Sartorises. Thus in *Flags in the Dust*, the presence of Colonel John Sartoris, who has been long dead, and that of his brother, Bayard I, pervade the entire novel and the modern-day Sartorises seem to live in the shadow of the past greatnesses of the Sartorises.

Several more characters from *The Unvanquished* also appear in Faulkner's other novels. Uncle Buck McCaslin and Uncle Buddy, for example, become central characters in *Go Down, Moses*, 1942, and the same type of radical social philosophy that was discussed in *The Unvanquished* is further developed in that novel.

In the story "Skirmish at Sartoris," we hear about Colonel Sartoris killing two carpetbaggers in order to keep the blacks from voting. There, the episode is told from the viewpoint of Bayard

Sartoris. In an earlier novel, *Light in August*, 1932, we hear the same episode narrated by a relative of the murdered men. Joanna Burden is the granddaughter and half-sister of the murdered men, and she explains how her relatives were only trying to raise up the status of the blacks. In still another story ("A Rose for Emily"), we hear about John Sartoris's paying the taxes anonymously for an aristocratic lady who has no money. He gallantly conceals his generosity and tells her that the city council exempted her of all taxes. *Absalom, Absalom!*, 1936, concerns Colonel Henry Sutpen, who was voted colonel of the regiment when Clonel Sartoris was voted out, and in *The Unvanquished*, Colonel Sartoris challenges him to a duel when Colonel Sutpen will not join the night riders. In *The Unvanquished*, Mrs. Compson, a minor character, is instrumental in getting Drusilla Hawk, an important character, married; not surprisingly, the Compson family is the subject of an entire novel, *The Sound and the Fury*, 1929. In addition, Ab Snopes, as will be noted below, is the progenitor of a family that will occupy three novels and many short stories.

Consequently, the mere creation of a mythological county in which characters from one novel appear and then reappear in other novels is, in itself, a highly imaginative and creative accomplishment. No other author has created anything that equals it in modern literature.

For some critics, however, the characterizations are not always consistent. For example, the Bayard Sartoris we see at the end of *The Unvanquished* (in "An Odor of Verbena") is a highly courageous young man with strong moral convictions. Yet in *Flags in the Dust*, the same Bayard Sartoris is in his seventies. It is hard for some people to imagine that the young Bayard of *The Unvanquished* could have developed into the type of Bayard whom they see in *Flags in the Dust*. I, personally, dismiss such criticism as nonsense since no one knows what a twenty-four-year-old person will be like when he is in his seventies.

If, then, throughout the Yoknapatawpha series, the name of Sartoris comes to represent the epitome of southern values — gallantry, generosity, valor, aristocracy, dedication to the ideals of the region, pride, and honor (in short, the essence of southern gentility and chivalry) — at the opposite pole of southern society are the Snopeses, with Ab Snopes being the progenitor of that clan. In *Flags in the Dust*, the Snopes family is mentioned as being a clan of hill people who gradually infiltrate every aspect of the town of Jefferson; it is here that Ab Snopes is mentioned as being the progenitor of that clan. Also in that novel, Faulkner shows various Snopeses involved in blackmail, embezzlement, draft dodging, and other shady deals. In a later novel, *Sanctuary*, more disreputable Snopeses appear in various, derogatory positions in Jefferson. *The Unvanquished*, then, presents an early picture of the father of this long line of Snopeses, a family which will ultimately become the main characters in Faulkner's famous trilogy (*The Hamlet*, *The Town*, and *The Mansion*), commonly referred to as The Snopes Trilogy. Ultimately, the Snopes family becomes synonymous with the rise of an amoral materialism which overpowers all other existing moral values. In Ab Snopes's wheedling, conniving, and lying, we see that those who descend from him will, by nature, represent the elemental and destructive forces of invincible rapacity which are opposed to all other forces of a decent and honorable society, such as the Sartoris family stands for.

The Sartoris family is honest in all its transactions, whether we approve of those transactions or not: Colonel Sartoris *did* confront the Burdens openly and *did* let the Burdens fire first; a Snopes would have sneaked up from behind and shot them. The Snopes family accomplishes its ends with a perverse and distorted vitality. Their ubiquitous inhumanity infiltrates every aspect of the community life, and their calculating and dehumanized exploitations leave their victims stupified and in abject rage. Separately, Ab Snopes's descendants are inveterate liars, thieves, murderers, and the personification of every type of treachery. As a clan, they present an insurmountable and invidious exemplification of the horrors of materialistic aggrandizement. While Colonel Sartoris and Granny Millard are trying to raise up the entire country, Ab Snopes and, later, his descendants would destroy anything for their own personal gain. Perhaps worst of all, however, the Snopeses are able to accomplish their aims with complete imperturbability. Ab Snopes shows no remorse over the death of Granny. When asked at the University of Virginia about the relationship between Ab Snopes and Grumby, Faulkner responded that Ab Snopes "was a hanger-on, he was a sort of jackal. Grumby in a way was a lion—he was a shabby, sorry lion—but Ab Snopes was never anything but a jackal, and I imagine that Grumby would have had little patience with Ab

Snopes. Ab Snopes hung around the outskirts of the kill to get what scraps might be left over."

Ultimately, all the Snopeses are so impersonal that their gruesome inhumanity can be viewed only in a comic fashion. We can't hate Ab Snopes. When he is caught by Bayard, he merely falls down in the mud and whines. The whipping he receives has no significance to him other than the immediate pain. There are indeed later Snopeses that one can hate, but this one is more pathetic in his wheedling and whining than he is loathsome. As a result, the Snopeses have lent their name to a modern social disease called Snopesism, a term which has come to mean an unprincipled, amoral materialism. It is, therefore, another measure of Faulkner's genius that he has created such vivid characterizations of the Snopeses that the modern, cultured, literary world uses their name to describe a modern illness of society.

In conclusion, *The Unvanquished* presents us with two of the dominant families of Yoknapatawpha County; the Sartoris family represents the most noble aspects of humanity, while the Snopes clan represents the worst aspects of humanity.

LIST OF CHARACTERS

PRINCIPAL CHARACTERS: *these characters are discussed in further detail in other parts of the Notes, as will be indicated.*

Bayard Sartoris

The narrator of all the stories; he is twelve years old in the first story, and he matures during the course of all the stories. In the final story, he is twenty-four years old. For further discussion, see the Character Analyses section.

Colonel John Sartoris

Bayard's father, whom he admires in spite of recognizing many of his flaws. The Colonel is voted out of his regiment and replaced by Colonel Sutpen; Colonel Sartoris then returns to Yoknapatawpha County and raises a troop of irregulars. For further discussion, see the Character Analyses section, plus the Yoknapatawpha County section.

Granny (Miss Rosa Millard)

Colonel John Sartoris's mother-in-law; she takes care of and manages the Sartoris mansion during the Colonel's absence. She is beloved by the entire county for her humanitarian treatment of all of the citizens—black and white. For further discussion, see the Character Analyses section.

Ringo

During the early stories, Ringo is the constant Negro companion and equal of Bayard Sartoris. Both boys are the same age and both nursed from Ringo's mother's breasts. As the boys grow older, the South's attitude toward Ringo's color becomes increasingly important until in the last story, the color line between the two young men has become a vast social gulf. For further explanation, see the Character Analyses section and the discussion of "An Odor of Verbena."

Drusilla Hawk Sartoris

When her fiancé is killed in one of the early battles of the Civil War, Drusilla discards her feminine clothes, dresses like a man, and rides with Colonel John Sartoris's troops as one of the common soldiers. Later, she is forced to marry John Sartoris, even though she lives innocently in the same cabin with him and Bayard while attempting to help them reconstruct the ruined Sartoris plantation. For further discussion, see the Character Analyses section.

Ab Snopes

While telling people that he is following the instructions of Colonel Sartoris to look after the "womenfolk," he is, in actuality, avoiding all contact with the war. He wheedles his way into Granny's lucrative mule trading business, not to help the people, but for personal gain. For further discussion, see the Yoknapatawpha County section.

LESSER OR MINOR CHARACTERS: *this section makes no attempt to cover every character who is named or mentioned. For example, such a character as* **Celia Cook**, *the girl who scratches her name on the windowpane when General Forrest rides down the streets of Jefferson, has little or no significance. Likewise,* **Judge Benbow** *is mentioned only once; he arranges the sale of the railroad between Redmond and Colonel Sartoris. All of the characters listed below, however, have some significant functions in the novel's totality. They appear in alphabetical order, rather than in their order of importance.*

Cassius Q. Benbow (Cash)

In "Skirmish at Sartoris," he is the Negro that the carpetbaggers are trying to elect as U.S. Marshal; the prevention of his election is one of the main concerns of the story.

Matt Bowden and Bridger

Matt Bowden is the person who first tries to get Bayard and Ringo to give up their search for Grumby, and later he and Bridger are the two people who hand Grumby over to Bayard and Ringo.

Gavin Breckbridge

Drusilla Hawk's fiancé, whose death at the battle of Shiloh causes her to turn into a woman bent on revenge against the Yankees.

The Burdens

Their first names are never given, but from other sources, we know that the two are Grandfather Calvin Burden I and his grandson, Calvin Burden II. In "Skirmish at Sartoris," they are presented as carpetbaggers trying to organize the Negroes into a voting bloc. Both are shot and killed by Colonel Sartoris.

Mrs. Compson

A member of one of the most prominent families in the county; she is a friend of Miss Rosa Millard and is one of the ladies who is instrumental in getting Drusilla married. Her husband is considered eccentric since his favorite pastime is shooting sweet potatoes off the heads of Negro children. She appears, or is mentioned, in all of the stories in this volume, except "Ambuscade."

Colonel Nathaniel G. Dick

Although his name is not mentioned when he first appears, he is the Yankee colonel who orders his men to stop their search of the Sartoris house in "Ambuscade," even though he knows the two boys are hiding under Granny's skirts. Later, in "Raid," he is the man who authorizes the return of the mules and silverware to Granny.

Aunt Jenny Du Pre (née Virginia Sartoris)

Aunt Jenny appears only in the last story. She is Colonel Sartoris's sister; her husband was killed during the war. Faulkner comments that her eyes are wise and tolerant; proof of this is when she supports Bayard's decision not to kill Ben Redmond.

Brother Fortinbride

He was an enlisted man in Colonel Sartoris's regiment, but when he was wounded, he was sent home to die. He recovered, however, and became a preacher, helping Granny distribute money and mules to the poor people in the story "Riposte in Tertio"; in "Vendée," he preaches Granny's funeral sermon.

Grumby

The vicious leader of a group of raiders who prey upon unprotected women and children by riding up and down the land,

16

pillaging and destroying everything in sight. He kills Granny in "Riposte in Tertio" and, in turn, is hunted down and killed by Bayard and Ringo in "Vendeé."

Mrs. Habersham (Martha)

In "Skirmish at Sartoris," she is the person most instrumental in trying to get John Sartoris and Drusilla Hawk married, even though the marriage does not take place until after the story ends.

Dennison Hawk, Jr. (Cousin Denny)

He is Drusilla's ten-year-old brother, whom we first meet in "Raid," when he tells of his sister's encounter with the Yankees over her horse, Bobolink. In "An Odor of Verbena," Drusilla leaves to join Denny in Montgomery, where he is "reading law" (studying to be a lawyer).

Louisa Hawk (infrequently referred to as Louise Hawk)

Drusilla's mother; she is convinced that her daughter has brought shame to the family by her wild, unfeminine actions, and she demands that Colonel Sartoris marry Drusilla. She appears in "Raid," is mentioned in "Riposte in Tertio," and is central to "Skirmish at Sartoris."

Joby

Ringo's grandfather; he served as Colonel Sartoris's body servant and is present in all the stories. He is married to Louvinia; their son is Simon. He grumbles over the many tasks assigned to him, but along with Louvinia, he is fiercely loyal to the Sartoris family.

Loosh

He is Joby's son; he figures prominently in "Ambuscade," where he seems to know more about the war than even the white people. He becomes involved in the freedom movement and leaves the Sartoris plantation after showing the Yankees where the silverware is hidden. After the war, however, he returns to the Sartoris homeplace. He appears in all the stories except "Vendée" and "Skirmish at Sartoris."

Louvinia

Joby's wife; she is a loyal servant of the Sartoris family and she appears in all the stories. She expresses her disgust with her son Loosh because of his bold, arrogant behavior.

Uncle Buck (Theophilus) McCaslin and Uncle Buddy (Amodeus) McCaslin

Twin brothers who both want to join the southern cause, but since they are seventy years old, it is decided that only one of them can go off to war; the other must remain at home. They play a game of poker to see which one goes; Uncle Buddy wins and, thus, Uncle Buck has to stay at home. He assists Bayard and Ringo when they track down Grumby, Granny's murderer, in "Vendée." Earlier, in "Retreat," we heard about Uncle Buck and Uncle Buddy's unusual social philosophy concerning the land and the freeing of the slaves. Uncle Buck is mentioned in several of the other stories, but does not appear in them.

Colonel G. W. Newberry

The Yankee colonel from Illinois from whom Granny gets her last batch of mules in "Riposte in Tertio."

Philadelphy

Loosh's wife; she feels that she is obliged to go with her husband when he leaves the Sartoris family. She is one of the Negroes that Granny goes searching for in "Raid."

Ben Redmond

In "An Odor of Verbena," he is Colonel Sartoris's partner during the building of the railroad, but when the two of them cannot agree any longer, each offers a price to buy the other out. Redmond asks a price, certain that Colonel Sartoris cannot raise that amount of money, but the Colonel *is* able to raise it and, therefore, he buys the railroad at a price far below its worth. When Redmond runs for the legislature, Colonel Sartoris runs against him, just for spite, and soundly defeats him. Later, he goads Redmond so frequently and so badly that even Colonel Sartoris's closest friends try to stop him. Finally, for a reason we never learn, Redmond kills Colonel Sartoris. When Bayard goes to confront Redmond unarmed, Redmond fires two shots at an intentional, wrong angle, then walks through a crowd of men, boards a train, leaves Jefferson, and is never heard of again.

Colonel Henry Sutpen

Originally, Colonel Sutpen was second in command of the regiment that Colonel Sartoris had raised. When the regiment votes Colonel Sartoris out of command, after the second battle at Manassas, Sutpen is elected to lead the regiment. After the war, he refuses to join the night riders, organized by Colonel Sartoris. When Colonel Sartoris challenges him to a duel, Sutpen turns his back and walks away, maintaining that every man should go home and look after his own land. He appears only in "An Odor of Verbena."

Professor and Mrs. Wilkins

This is the couple with whom Bayard Sartoris is living when Ringo arrives with the news that Colonel Sartoris has been killed (see "An Odor of Verbena"). Professor Wilkins offers Bayard his gun, but Bayard refuses to take it.

George Wyatt

A member of Colonel Sartoris's troop of irregulars; he is immensely loyal to the Colonel, and he is enthusiastic over the Colonel's killing of the carpetbaggers in "Skirmish at Sartoris." In "An Odor of Verbena," he gathers other members of the Colonel's old troop of irregulars to support Bayard when Bayard goes in to Jefferson to confront Redmond.

19

SARTORIS GENEALOGY

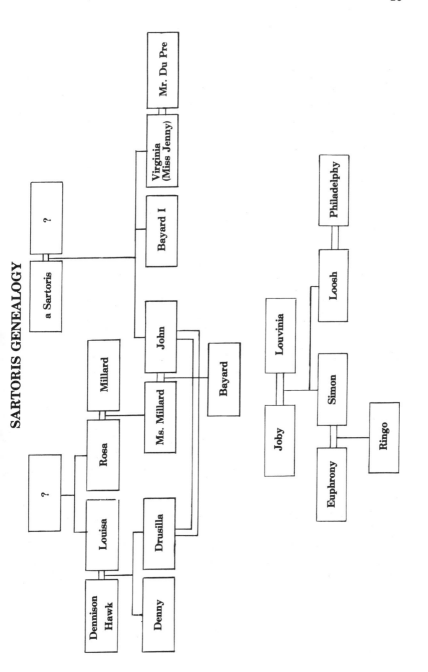

CRITICAL COMMENTARIES

AMBUSCADE

The title of this story means "to lie in wait in the woods" or "to ambush"; by old chivalric codes of honor, then, the title carries a negative connotation because in olden times no real soldier would stoop so low as to ambush his enemy. In the title of the first story of this collection, Faulkner is warning the reader that the entire series of stories might be an *ambush* on the values embedded in southern society. There is nothing noble, for example, about lying in ambush to kill a Yankee who is trying to free members of the human race held in enslavement.

The novel, and particularly this first story, begins with a simple plot, but this seemingly simple plot disguises the larger meanings of the novel. Had Faulkner intended the story to be truly a simple one, he would have named it simply "Ambush," but by using a more archaic form of the word, he is calling attention to the fact that the entire Civil War was fought because of archaic issues—that is, what society can survive as a society when it fights so heroically for the enslavement of another race of people? Should we praise the heroism of the battle or should we examine the underlying principles governing the war?

As a framework for these deep, philosophical concerns, Faulkner uses a multitude of plain, homespun, over-simple pleasures and actions, and he lulls us into believing that the Civil War was filled with fun and games. Significantly, he never removes the reader from this romantic view in the first story; he narrates it in terms of its being a marvellous story of war and adventure, seen through the eyes of a young twelve-year-old boy. Deceptively, Faulkner is de-emphasizing the serious aspects of the war—the deaths, the destruction, the privations, and so forth—by revealing its romantic aspects. With this method, Faulkner evokes myths about the whole concept of war, myths that began with Homer's *Iliad*, when Achilles sulked childishly in his tent and refused to play the game of war for quite some time. In fact, the entire *Iliad* is interspersed with games of war and games of athletic prowess.

To open the novel, Faulkner uses an ironic situation: he presents the narrator, Bayard Sartoris, playing a game of war with Ringo, a black slave boy who is the same age as Bayard. The actual war is far away from them and, in historical fact, Vicksburg has already fallen, as we learn later from Loosh, Ringo's uncle. This is Faulkner's way of indicating that the Civil War is not just beginning; it is at a critical moment for the South. Here, Bayard and Ringo are in the process of reconstructing the battle by using a "handful of chips" from the woodpile to represent Vicksburg and a "trench scraped into the packed earth" for the Mississippi River. However, the river, through Faulkner's narrative, becomes more than just a trench; it lives: ". . . possessing even in miniature that ponderable though passive recalcitrance of topography which outweighs artillery, against which the most brilliant of victories and the most tragic of defeats are but the loud noises of a moment." The miniature Vicksburg is merely part of a game which the boys are playing, but the entirety of this first story focuses on games, the games that the young boys constantly play. These games, however, change drastically during the course of the novel, and thus the entire novel should be seen as a record of the growth and maturation of a young twelve-year-old boy. We witness his coming of age—as he relishes the make-believe violence of the childish games he plays in the first story, to his recognition of the need to hunt and kill and avenge his grandmother's death, and, finally, his rejection of violence in favor of law and order in the final story.

The first section of "Ambuscade," then, presents the games that Bayard and Ringo play; the two boys are involved in their war games when Loosh suddenly brings an element of reality into the game. With one sweep of his hand, Loosh destroys the entire Vicksburg "play-enforcement." Here, an alien element is introduced; just prior to Loosh's appearance, Bayard and Ringo were pretending that they were fighting "against a common enemy." With Loosh's action, we realize that the enemy is not so easy to determine for a black person since the war is concerned with the liberation of the blacks. It is, however, important to note that throughout these stories, Ringo, as a black, has adopted the values of the southern white code and will constantly be found siding with the Sartoris point of view, even until the last story, when he too feels the need to avenge the death of Colonel John Sartoris.

After Loosh leaves, hinting that he knows something about the war that the young boys do not know, Bayard and Ringo continue playing their war games, with Ringo playing a southern general, General Pemberton, and Bayard having to take his turn playing a northern general, General Grant. They have to take turns "even though Ringo was a nigger . . . because Ringo and I had been born in the same month and had both fed at the same breast and had slept together and eaten together for so long that Ringo called Granny 'Granny' just like I did."

In the midst of their games, Bayard's father, Colonel Sartoris, rides up. After greeting the two boys and sending his horse off to be curried, Bayard notes that his father "was not big; it was just the things he did, that we knew he was doing, had been doing in Virginia and Tennessee, that made him seem big to us." Here, Faulkner's purpose is especially clear: the first part of "Ambuscade" combines the play of the war games with Loosh introducing a hint of the real war and, finally, the real war is brought into focus with the return of Colonel Sartoris.

In Part 2 of "Ambuscade," Bayard tells us that Colonel Sartoris, with the help of Joby, Loosh, Ringo, and himself, is building a stock pen in the swamp so cleverly that no one will be able to find it. He also tells us that when the Colonel takes off his coat, he is surprised to see that he is wearing a pair of Yankee trousers which he took from a captured Yankee. He then continues his narrative: after they have completed building the stock pen, they return to the house and discover one of the big trunks from the attic sitting in the kitchen; they also discover that the table is set with kitchen knives and forks—the silver service is missing. After supper, the boys anxiously wait to hear stories about the war; the Colonel is a good storyteller, and they anticipate hearing him tell about the cannon fire and flags waving and wild yelling, like he did two years ago, but the boys are sent to bed instead. They don't go all the way upstairs, however; they sit for awhile on the stairs and listen to the Colonel give instructions to Loosh to get shovels and lanterns and to meet him later. Ringo is sure that they are going to bury the silver. When the boys awaken the next morning, both the trunk filled with the silver service and the Colonel are gone.

This section focuses on the war's advancing closer to the boys' home. Yet neither one of them is fully aware of this fact. Two years ago, the Colonel had time to sit around and tell stories about the war to amuse the boys. Now he has no time for this. The front lines of the war are too close to home; there is no longer time for telling amusing stories and there are no amusing stories. The fall of Vicksburg and the impending arrival of the enemy upon the actual soil of the Sartoris plantation are imminent. In fact, the Yankees are so close that it is necessary to hide the stock in the swamp and to bury the silverware. But in the midst of all this, there is still an element of mystery and fun for the boys. The grim actuality of war itself is still far away.

This section also tells us more about Colonel Sartoris. He is not a stereotypical southern colonel—formal, distant, and reserved; instead, he is willing to remove his jacket and participate, alongside the black slaves, in the physical work of building the stock pen. And while the Colonel can suddenly and mysteriously appear out of the woods, he can also suddenly disappear. Yet his character is firmly grounded in reality, particularly as we noted in the scene where he works and sweats along with the others to build the stock pen. Also in this section, we hear about the Colonel's library, a room which tells us a good deal about its owner. In the Colonel's library, there is a combination of intellectual books dealing with law and theories of law and justice, alongside the novels of Sir Walter Scott (dealing with romantic chivalry), as well as those of James Fenimore Cooper and Alexander Dumas, both writers of romantic fiction.

Part 3 of "Ambuscade" opens the day after the Colonel has left. Granny is telling Ringo to get the cookbook for her to read from because Ringo has asked her to read about "Cokynut cake"; Ringo is curious about coconut cake because he is not sure whether or not he has actually tasted it. Later, Bayard wants to secretly watch Loosh because in a dream he was told that Loosh knows things—". . . that he [Loosh] would know before we did . . . [and] if we watched him, we could tell by what he did when it was getting ready to happen." Bayard and Ringo watch Loosh, and one night he leaves and does not return until later the next night. Then he announces to the other slaves that they are going to be set free. The other slaves do not believe him, but Ringo and Bayard do, and they decide that they should start watching the road for any approaching Yankees. After two days, they spot a Yankee on horseback, and they return to the manor house and take down an old musket from over the fireplace. Then they return to where they saw the Yankee. With great difficulty, they work together and manage to fire the old musket and discover that it is not a single soldier coming around the curve in the road: it is "the whole army!"

In this section, Faulkner presents the central action of the story—the ambush of the Yankee soldier. First, he continues his lighthearted tone as he describes Granny reading about "Cokynut cake," but simultaneously we realize that there is a serious dimension even in this comic episode: the war has stopped all possibility of the Sartoris family having access to such a thing as coconut. The narrative then focuses on the fact that Loosh does indeed know things that the others do not know. Yet Loosh's report that the Yankees are coming to free the slaves does not have any true social significance for the two boys; instead, Loosh's news is merely the reason why they start watching the road for Yankees to actually start arriving. Ironically, Bayard even assumes that if Ringo is freed, then he too will be freed. Later he asks Ringo, "Do you want to be free?" We realize at this point that neither Bayard nor Ringo has any real concept of why the war is being fought. Their actual firing on the Yankee, however, takes the action away from the element of play and games and brings the reality of war into the boys' immediate situation.

Section 4 continues the narrative as the young boys flee to Granny for protection after they shoot at the Yankee. Granny, fearing that they have actually killed a man and seeing Yankee soldiers approaching the house, hides the two boys under her billowing skirts. When the Yankee sergeant demands to know where the two boys are, Granny tells a lie—for her, a grave sin. "There are," she says, "no children in this house nor on this place. There is no one here at all except my servant and myself and the people in the quarters." The sergeant sends some of his men to search the house, and Granny questions him about the man who was killed; she is greatly relieved to discover that it was only a horse and not a man, even a Yankee, that was killed. A Yankee colonel enters the house, learns of the situation, and is instantly aware that Granny has hidden the two boys under her skirts, yet he refuses to confront the lady with the truth. He has the sergeant call off his men and, after a bit more conversation (during which he makes it clear that he knows Granny is lying), he and his men leave. Granny rises from her chair, kneels down to pray for forgiveness for having lied, and then sends the boys to the kitchen for soap since they used a curse word earlier.

Section 5 closes the story with Bayard's recollection of having his mouth washed out with soap. He remembers spitting out soap bubbles and their disappearing, a metaphor for the disappearance of many other things in the past. Obviously, however, Bayard has never forgotten Granny nor her unique sense of morality. In this particular story, she utters her first lie; later, as the novel continues, she will gradually become enmeshed in a tissue of lies and deception which will cause her death. Here, as later, her lie is practical—its purpose is to protect her grandchild and his Negro playmate; all her lies will be practical, but they will result, nonetheless, in her death.

Granny's code of southern ethics is one that values honor and integrity, and she trusts others to believe in the same things—even the Yankees. If they happen to be gentlemen, they are to be trusted as gentlemen. The code of the South is one which allows Granny to believe that her cause (the southern cause) is correct and that God is, of course, on her side. As a result, she is sorry that she lied, but she did so in order to protect the boys and also to uphold the principle of slavery; such things can ultimately be forgiven. But she firmly adheres to that part of the southern code which does *not* allow young children to use obscenity; consequently, she washes out her grandson's mouth with soap as a punishment for swearing.

The Yankee colonel is never identified in this particular story, but later we will discover that he is Colonel Dick, and Granny will go to find him in order to retrieve the Sartoris silverware and mules. Later, this seemingly trivial encounter with a stranger, albeit a Yankee "gentleman" colonel, will be a factor in the circumstances of Granny's death. As Ringo will comment later, "It was those first mules that caused her death."

"Ambuscade," as we have noted, will seem on first reading to be a simple story; indeed, it will seem to be the simplest story in the novel. In one sense it is, but at the same time it is also one of the most unified stories in the collection—that is, it deals with one single episode, and its characters, its actions, and its mood are all pivotal to the entire novel.

RETREAT

Of all the individual stories in *The Unvanquished*, "Retreat" is the most diffused and the least unified; even though it is divided into only two parts, it nevertheless deals with several significant events without ever bringing them into a unified whole. In the first section, which occurs about a year after the events in "Ambuscade," Colonel Sartoris has apparently told Miss Rosa Millard to take the family's sterling silverware to Memphis. We do not witness these instructions being given; we draw this conclusion later, after the story begins, on the night before Granny, Bayard, Ringo, and Joby leave for Memphis. They are making preparations to leave early the next morning, and the trunkful of silver, which they buried a year ago, has to be dug up in spite of the fact that all of the blacks feel that it would be safer to leave it where it is and dig it up just before leaving. But Granny insists that the trunk be dug up now; she had had a dream in which a black man went to where the trunk was buried in the orchard and stood pointing at it, revealing its whereabouts. She refuses to tell the others which particular black man it was, but Bayard and Ringo know which one she means: Granny is referring to Loosh. Recall that in "Ambuscade," Granny's son-in-law, Colonel Sartoris, told Bayard in a dream "to watch Loosh, because he knows." It was not until the end of the story, however, that Faulkner revealed to us what the Colonel sensed earlier. Loosh is not stupid; he listens and tries to make some sense of what is happening. It was Loosh, in "Ambuscade," who told the Sartoris slaves that the Yankees were going to free them, a fact which the majority of the blacks could not fully understand. In contrast, the idea of being freed fascinates Loosh, and Granny does not trust him for that reason. Bayard and Ringo realize this and, therefore, they both instantly know whom Granny is referring to when Louvinia tries her best to make Granny tell which of the blacks she believes will betray the family. Clearly, Granny is referring to Loosh.

After Joby and Loosh dig up the trunk, Granny insists that they take it all the way upstairs to her bedroom, in spite of the fact that they will have to take it downstairs again in the morning and load it on the wagon.

The second section of the story, a long section, covers several different episodes. It begins the next morning after Granny, Joby, Bayard, and Ringo have finished breakfast and are preparing to leave. The trunk filled with silver is brought downstairs, loaded on the wagon, and they all set out—leaving the Sartoris plantation, stopping by the Compsons's place, and then continuing on to Jefferson, where they are stopped by Uncle Buck McCaslin. Faulkner's first digression from the plot line concerns a brief history of the McCaslin twins. He tells us about Uncle Buck and Uncle Buddy, two old bachelors in their seventies who try an experiment with their Negroes: they let them work for their freedom—that is, they pay for it with their work on the plantation. We also learn in this digression that when Colonel Sartoris started to raise his first regiment, Uncle Buck and Uncle Buddy both wanted to volunteer, but since they were too old, it was decided that a game of draw poker would decide who would go. In fact, they threatened to raise their own regiment against the Colonel's regiment if at least one of them could not go. Uncle Buddy won the poker game and went to fight the Yankees, and thus it is Uncle Buck who meets Bayard and Ringo on the streets of Jefferson this day, shaking his walking stick at them and, in the same breath, simultaneously damning the Colonel and canonizing his efforts in the war.

After this digression, Faulkner returns to his story line and focuses again on Bayard and Ringo as they pick up Miss Rosa at the Compson place, where she stopped to get some rose cuttings to take along to Memphis. Then they set out, beginning a long journey. The days are fairly uneventful until the fourth day; then they encounter a Confederate regiment, and the officer in charge tries to convince them that they will never reach Memphis. The countryside is rampant with Yankee patrols, all of whom would be delighted to capture some kinfolk of the notorious Colonel Sartoris and hold them for ransom. However, Granny is neither frightened nor persuaded to turn back, and they continue on their way until they encounter—almost immediately—a group of Yankees. The wild, yelling soldiers pull out their pocket knives, cut the mules loose from the wagon, and ride off. Bayard and Ringo try to follow the Yankees, who are herding the captured Sartoris mules, while Granny is left sitting with Joby in the muleless wagon.

Bayard and Ringo run toward a house, "borrow" a horse, and follow the Yankees until it is dark; they fall asleep under a bridge and the next morning they find themselves surrounded by horses and men. At first, they are terrified until they recognize Jupiter, Colonel Sartoris's horse, and they realize that they are surrounded by the Colonel and his men.

As Colonel Sartoris is escorting the boys back to the Sartoris plantation, they suddenly ride upon an encampment of about sixty Yankees; Sartoris's innovative reaction is superb: he pretends to have a large number of troops surrounding the Yankees and yells commands to his make-believe lieutenants, demanding the surrender of the Yankees. Afterward, he takes their food and their rifles and makes them strip down to their underwear. He then pretends to relax so as to allow the prisoners to escape in small groups in their underwear. This way, the Yankees think that they have outwitted Colonel Sartoris and his "regiment"; they never realize that the Colonel has only a few men with him.

As Sartoris and the boys arrive back at the Sartoris plantation, they see Granny returning on the wagon with the trunkful of silver and some "borrowed" horses; later, they bury the silverware in the same place where they had dug it up some days previously.

After finishing a day's work, Colonel Sartoris is relaxing, sitting on the front porch with his stocking feet propped up on the railing, when about fifty Yankees suddenly gallop up to the front door. The Colonel sends Ringo out to the barn to saddle his horse, and he sends Bayard into the house to tell Louvinia to get his boots and pistols ready at the back door. The Colonel then pretends to be old, infirm, and "born loony." He goes into the house ostensibly to get his boots, under the pretext of leading the Yankees to where Colonel Sartoris is, but he runs to the barn, jumps on his horse, and escapes before the Yankees realize what has happened.

After his escape, Granny discovers that the Yankees have set fire to the house and, at the same moment, she also realizes that Loosh has shown the Yankees where the silver is buried. Furthermore, Loosh is now leaving the plantation, proclaiming: "I done been freed; God's own angel proclamated me free and gonter general me to Jordan. I don't belong to John Sartoris now; I belongs to me and God." When asked about the silver, Loosh maintains that he has as much right to give someone else's silver away as did that man who originally gave him to John Sartoris. Granny pleads with Loosh's wife, Philadelphy, not to go, but Philadelphy feels that she must: "He be my husband. I reckon I got to go with him." The story closes with the silver being carried away by the Yankees, the blacks fleeing, the house burning, and Miss Rosa, Bayard, and Ringo all crying out together, "The bastuds! . . . The bastuds! The bastuds!"

As was stated earlier, the reason why Granny is going to Memphis with Bayard and Ringo is never fully stated in this story and might be confusing to some readers. But as we review the story in its entirety, Faulkner explains—in digressions—that Colonel Sartoris was the first person in Yoknapatawpha County to raise a regiment of soldiers himself. From Uncle Buck McCaslin, we learn that the regiment later voted Colonel Sartoris out of command and elected another person (his name is not mentioned here, but in "An Odor of Verbena," we find out that this man is Colonel Thomas Sutpen). After he was relieved of his command, Colonel Sartoris returned to Jefferson and formed a company of irregulars. Consequently, to the enemy, Colonel Sartoris is not an official part of the Confederate Army; instead, he is something of a renegade outlaw who does not consider himself under the command of any other person. Also, we hear that there is a large reward offered for his capture. Knowing this, the Colonel is aware of the importance of having all of his kinfolk removed from the country; the Yankees are moving in and they could easily take revenge upon Bayard and Miss Rosa. To prevent this, he sends them to Memphis, and they take the silver with them because Miss Rosa believes that Loosh will eventually reveal its whereabouts to the Yankees, as indeed he does at the end of the story.

In this story, we are also introduced to the McCaslin twins (to Uncle Buck, directly, and we hear indirectly about Uncle Buddy). These two characters will become major figures in one of Faulkner's later novels, *Go Down, Moses*. These brothers advocate a type of social philosophy which is radically humanitarian, in contrast to many of the beliefs of the South. First of all, they believe that "land did not belong to people but that people belonged to land and that the earth would permit them to live on and out of it and use it only so long as they behaved and that if they did not behave right, it would shake them off just like a dog getting rid of fleas." These ideas are further developed in *Go Down, Moses*. Even more radical for the time, however, is the McCaslins' system of allowing their slaves to earn their freedom by "buying it not in money . . . but in work from the plantation." Yet as contradictory as these ideas are to the rest of the citizens of the South, Uncle Buck and Uncle Buddy are, nevertheless, fiercely loyal southerners who fight for the rights of the South—even though they disagree with the prevalant concepts involved in slavery. Their independence involves a deep resentment that any other part of the nation can force its ways of thinking and acting upon the South.

The comic, tense episode during which Colonel Sartoris surrounds a large number of Yankees and makes them surrender to his handful of men shows us, firsthand, the ingenuity and the mythic greatness of Colonel Sartoris—how he won his reputation for bravery and bravura. He is clearly skilled in the ways of warfare, and he possesses the accompanying skills necessary for a successful fighter, in addition to having the determination to accomplish whatever he sets out to do.

The theme of "borrowing" is beginning to take on added significance in this story. Bayard and Ringo "borrow" the old horse that they ride on, and when Granny comes back to the Sartoris plantation, she won't answer questions about where she got the horses she is driving; she will say only that she "borrowed" them. However, when the Yankees "borrow" the Sartoris' silver, it is entirely a different matter. Yet all this "borrowing" will lead to the business of "borrowing" large numbers of mules from the Yankees in the next two stories and will culminate in Granny's violent death.

At the very end of this story, after Granny returns home with the stolen horses, Bayard and Ringo have also come home on stolen horses, yet Granny is at a loss to understand why Loosh would betray the hiding place of the Sartoris silver. When Loosh announces his freedom, Granny reminds him that the "silver belongs to John Sartoris. . . . Who are you to give it away?" It is then that Loosh answers her: "Let God ax John Sartoris who the man name that give me to him. Let the man that buried me in the black dark ax that of the man what dug me free." Once again, Faulkner illustrates the inability of the southern white to understand the black man's need for freedom or even the black man's sense of his own humanity. Granny is too completely a product of the southern society of her time to recognize any type of individual need for freedom for the black man.

As a minor point, but one that should not be missed, note that at the end of "Ambuscade" the boys had their mouths washed out with soap for saying "bastud"; now, amidst the burning of the Sartoris manor house, all three—Ringo, Bayard and Granny—all say it, three times: "The bastuds! . . . The bastuds! The bastuds!"

RAID

Whereas the first two stories of this novel were tied together by the pranks and the childish games of Bayard and Ringo, the third story introduces the concept which will ultimately cause the death of Granny, Miss Rosa. The Sartoris house has been burned; the Sartoris mules, the family's silverware, and two Negroes have been taken (confiscated or stolen) by the Yankees, and Granny, Bayard, and Ringo set out on a long journey to recover these properties. In the process, Granny is given a document signed by a Yankee general which will ultimately become the instrument responsible for her death. The concept of whether something is borrowed or stolen or confiscated is intertwined with many of the actions in this story. The horses which they are driving, for example, are "borrowed," and this story and the next one, "Riposte in Tertio," deal with Granny's "borrowing"—requisitioning illegally—and using Yankee mules (many of which have been confiscated from the southerners) in order to help the poor, struggling people in Granny's own Yoknapatawpha County.

In conjunction with the above, Faulkner attempts in this story an almost impossible task. He wants to communicate and convey a sense of the horrors and the chaos caused by the war. He wants to show the destruction and confusion that accompanies the various aspects of the war. Furthermore, he wants to show the huge, homeless masses of black people, who have just been given their freedom, wandering aimlessly around the countryside, looking for the fabled River Jordan of biblical tales. At the same time, he shows us the burned houses throughout the land and the destroyed railroad tracks. He shows us a bridge being blown up by the Yankees, regardless of the potential deaths of many black people whom the Yankees are supposedly fighting to free. In other words, the story captures the horrors attendant on any war and the various effects which it wreaks on large groups of people and on individual members of society. The total effect of the story is that of disunity and confusion. And yet, all of these serious episodes are narrated through the eyes of a young boy who does not see the literal horrors of war; instead, he sees more often than not the humorous aspects of his and Granny's and Ringo's adventures in a war-torn countryside.

"Raid" is divided into three parts, and each part further

develops Granny's concept of honor and her allegiance to the values of the old South, which will influence most of her actions.

In the first section, Granny will not allow Ringo and Bayard to use the "borrowed" horses to go into town to Mrs. Compson's to borrow her hat, her parasol, and her hand mirror. Yet in terms of the entire story and the story that follows, she will "borrow" about two hundred and forty-eight (the exact number might be a few more or a few less) horses and mules from the Yankees—and sell them *back* to the Yankees—so that she can "borrow" them back again. The reader must keep in mind that at the beginning of this story the Sartoris mansion has been burned to the ground and that most of the Negro slaves have wandered off to unknown places. There is absolute disorder and chaos upon the land, and the borrowing of the mules becomes more acceptable in this world turned upside down, this new world of disorder.

Granny cannot understand how the continuing, needless destruction by the Yankees and the burning of the Sartoris mansion is going to help the enemy win the war. The Yankees' logic is unfathomable. Yet she decides that she must endure even in this chaos—having no house to live in, having no food, and very little money. She must begin again and, thus, she and Bayard decide to go and live in the slave quarters, which were not burned and are now largely empty. In addition, Granny has a goal: to repossess the Sartoris things that were needlessly taken; for that reason, she and Bayard and Ringo set out for Alabama, where her sister, Louisa, lives and where Colonel Dick, the gentlemanly Yankee officer, is stationed. He is the officer who intervened at the end of "Ambuscade"; Granny considers him a "gentleman," regardless of which side of the war he is fighting on. She believes that because he is a gentleman, he will replace her stolen property. The purpose, then, of this journey is to retrieve the trunk of silverware, the Sartoris' two mules (Old Hundred and Tinney) and the Sartoris' two Negro slaves (Loosh and Philadelphy); however, by a fluke of misunderstanding, Granny returns home with far more than she hoped for, or bargained for. Actually, in terms of the first section of this story, the motivation for the trip to Alabama is never given, and it is only later in the story that we are able to conclude that Granny knew that Colonel Dick was stationed in that region.

Returning to the narrative, we read that after some six days on the road, Granny and the boys have passed so many burned houses and so much gruesome destruction that they know they are following the path of General Sherman, a Yankee general who is systematically and maniacally destroying everything that lies in his path. Later, Granny even blames him for leading all of the Negroes to what they believe is the River Jordan. As was noted, it is on this sixth day that a large group of vagabond blacks passes the wagon during the night. One black woman, carrying a baby, falls behind, and Granny stops the wagon. She hears the black woman say that she "couldn't keep up . . . and they went off and left me." Granny tries to make her go back "home," but is unsuccessful; she then asks if the woman's husband is with the group. Finally, she offers to let the black woman ride in the wagon, but later the black woman wants to get off the wagon. Ringo tells Granny that the woman thinks that she has found the group of blacks she is looking for—even though they can't see them. Ringo also says that he is sure that the black woman will "lose um again tonight. . . ."

It is ironic in this scene and in others like it that throughout the novel Granny will *act* as though she is a great humanitarian, when, in fact, she considers the Negroes to be no more or no less than slaves. She will share her food with them, give them rides, money, or help of any nature, but, at the same time, she will remain a lady of "the old order," one who cannot understand the concept of a black person desiring anything other than serving his white master. Several times, she tells the blacks to "go back home," not realizing how empty her advice is. For the blacks, now that they are free, what—and where—is "home"? To Granny, "home" means the plantations where they worked for their white owners. In each encounter with a black, Granny asks, "Who do you belong to?" Therefore, as a representative of "the old order" of the South, she is, in one sense, a humanitarian, yet she is, at the same time, totally incapable of understanding the causes which motivated the Civil War itself, and she contents herself, instead, with helping the individual, unfortunate human beings she encounters—black or white—to survive in a time of destruction and chaos.

After the sixth day of their journey, Granny and the boys go past the graveyard, and Bayard sees the town of Hawkhurst, where Granny's sister lives. This is the place where Bayard had earlier seen the railroad, a mysterious marvel which Ringo has never seen. (This fact, for awhile, makes Bayard superior to Ringo.) As soon as they approach Louisa's house, they see Bayard's ten-year-old cousin, Denny, whose house has also been burned and who is now living in the slave quarters with his mother and with his sister, Drusilla. Immediately, Denny wants to take Bayard and Ringo to the railroad and show them what happened: the railroad ties were dug up and burned in a heap, and the steel rails were pried up and wrapped around trees.

The scene is unreal to Ringo; anticipating the chance to actually see a railroad and a locomotive, he is crushed when his dreams are suddenly shattered; finding the rails torn up, wrapped around trees, or gone altogether, Ringo's reaction reemphasizes on a simple level the contrast between the child's view of war and, on the other hand, the horrible destructive acts of war. For the boys, their simple dreams of might and magic, embodied in the locomotive and its shining steel tracks, have been destroyed. Yet in the larger sense, the destruction of the railroad represents the destruction of the entire southern culture—that is, for the members of "the old order," the war is rapidly becoming a lost cause.

While they are looking at the ruins of the railroad, Denny's sister, Drusilla, rides up on her prized horse, Bobolink. During the evening, Denny tells how Drusilla saved the horse from the Yankees. When they were going to take Bobolink by force, she put a pistol to the horse's head and told the Yankees, "I can't shoot you all, because I haven't enough bullets, and it wouldn't do any good anyway; but I won't need but one shot for the horse, and which shall it be?" After this confrontation, the Yankees let Drusilla keep the horse.

That night at the slave quarters, Drusilla tells them all about the night movement of the blacks and that the blacks believe that the river not far away is their chance for freedom; to the blacks, the river is like the River Jordan and, therefore, synonymous with freedom, salvation, and eternal happiness. Later in the night, the family goes outside and listens to the blacks pass by. Drusilla expresses her concern over their welfare. Aunt Louisa feels that "we cannot be responsible" for the fate of the blacks. If there are now thousands of them swarming about the river and on the bridge—which the Yankees plan to blow up—Aunt Louisa believes that "the Yankees brought it on themselves; let them pay the price." But Drusilla disagrees: "Those Negroes are not Yankees. . . ." Once again, this is a part of Faulkner's double structure of the novel, emphasizing the double standards that inform its entirety. Drusilla and Granny consider the blacks to be southerners, and Granny wants to protect and help them, but as we will see in "Skirmish at Sartoris," the Negroes must ultimately remain Negroes—that is, they can expect no rights even if, in theory, they are free. Later, for example, they cannot vote, even though they have been declared to be "free."

Drusilla, who lost her fiance in the war, is totally committed to the war effort. At bedtime, she tells Bayard that she no longer sleeps: "Why not stay awake now? Who wants to sleep now, with so much happening, so much to see? Living used to be dull, you see. Stupid." Drusilla then makes one of the most fantastic and incredible requests that any southern woman of that time might imagine: she tells Bayard, "When you go back home and see Uncle John, ask him to let me come there and ride with his troop. Tell him I can ride, and maybe I can learn to shoot." (Even though she calls Colonel Sartoris "Uncle John," there is no blood kinship between the two.)

Significantly, Drusilla, who is introduced in this story, will become one of Faulkner's strongest, most determined women and one of the most fierce defenders of "the old order" of the South. From the time we learn that her fiance was killed at Shiloh until Denny tells the story of her defying the Yankees, threatening to kill her horse Bobolink rather than let them take it, we see a woman who does not need or require sleep, one who spurns the ordinary things that ladies are expected to do and asserts her own brand of individualism. When she introduces the idea that she wants to ride with the soldiers—a thing unheard of in that society or virtually any other society in that time—we are prepared for a woman of strong principles. Historically, however, war has always been the business of men, not of women, and Faulkner further emphasizes the universality of the idea of war's being for men when he writes that "old men have been telling young men and boys about wars and fighting before they discovered how to write it down." In this passage, he is, of course, referring to the oldest piece of literature in Western civilization—Homer's *Iliad*, which deals with men in war. Consequently, Drusilla's desire to go ride with her "Uncle John" (he is later referred to by Drusilla as *Cousin* John in "Skirmish at Sartoris") has to be viewed as an act that transcends all regional customs since the beginning of time; this unheard of, shocking request sets her apart from all the other women in the novel. This request also prepares the reader for Drusilla's unusual role later in both "Skirmish at Sartoris" and "An Odor of Verbena."

The following day, Granny, Bayard, and Ringo leave with Drusilla to cross the river before the bridge is blown up in order to reach Colonel Dick, but there are such swarms of blacks converged around the river that, in the confusion of the crossing, the wagon is upset, and the horses are drowned. The entire narration of the river crossing emphasizes once again the absolute confusion associated with the war and its destructive power. The Yankees are determined to blow up the bridge—regardless of how many Negroes are on it or anywhere near it. Significantly, Granny is almost killed; in fact, there is so much chaos and confusion that Faulkner's narrative takes on added dramatic emphasis because it parallels the chaos he writes about. Using Bayard as his narrator, Faulkner is able to make us unsure what is actually happening and, therefore, the end of the second section of this story becomes an attempt to capture the utter confusion of one single episode associated with the total chaos of the war.

In the final section of the story, after the Yankees have helped recover the wagon from the river and have given Granny and the boys two of their own horses, Granny insists upon being taken to see Colonel Dick. Once there, Granny is promised that her property will be returned, along with the Negroes taken from her. Describing the lost property, Granny's southern speech confuses the Yankees; she describes the two mules, the two Negroes, and the chest of silver, and the comparison of her description with the orderly's written requisition is the source of a rich vein of humor in the story. "Loosh" becomes "loose"; "Philadelphy" becomes a city; "Old Hundred," the mule, becomes one hundred mules, and "Tenny" becomes ten mules, making some one hundred and ten mules. Ultimately, the orderly thinks that Granny means, besides the one hundred and ten mules, one hundred and ten Negroes and, in addition, ten chests of silver. Granny is also supplied with sufficient food to expedite her passage home—food, it should be noted, which she willingly shares with all of the Negroes.

When they are stopped by a cavalry of Yankee troops, Granny shows them the requisition papers; the officer mistakenly thinks that she has not been supplied with enough mules, and so he gives her forty-seven more mules. Ironically, Granny wants to acquire the extra mules so that none of the blacks will have to walk. Thus, again we have the ironic double vision of a woman who is willing to deceive for humanitarian reasons so as to ease the immediate pain of people she would permanently define as slaves. And throughout it all, Granny is determined to have her own way. Ringo expresses a key statement concerning her character. He says, "And don't yawl worry about Granny. She 'cide what she want and then she kneel down about ten seconds and tell God what she aim to do, and then she git up and do hit. And them that don't like hit can git outen the way or git trompled." This quality is the key to her greatness and, ultimately, it will be the cause of her death, when she confronts Grumby (the leader of a group of depraved renegades) against the advice of everyone.

In the final scene of the story, we have another example of the double values that have operated throughout the story. It was all right to take one hundred and ten mules because the piece of paper requisitioned that many mules and because many of the mules were stolen from southerners in the first place. Yet, since Granny and the boys eventually have one hundred and twenty-two mules, instead of one hundred and ten mules, illegally obtained, they must *all* kneel down and pray.

Basically, however, this story emphasizes the mass confusion caused by the war, and this confusion is best depicted in the river scene where the Negroes are wandering around lost, without any direction to their lives. The Negroes have seen their masters' houses burned by the Yankees and they have heard that they are free; blindly, they now try to correlate these events with the River Jordan and salvation. As a result, we realize that untold numbers of them are fleeing into the (unnamed) river, drowning in their attempt to find the "promised land."

The values of the entire South are reversed in this wartime story. In any war, the innocent suffer, of course. Here, Granny and the others wonder about the needless destruction and the needless loss of life which they witness; at the same time, both Granny and Drusilla are concerned for, and are very protective of, the Negroes. Yet neither of them ever conceives of the blacks as being anything other than slaves.

RIPOSTE IN TERTIO

The title of this short story refers to two fencing terms: a "riposte" is a quick thrust after a short parry, and "tertio" means to hold back in the third position. In this story, Bayard does not want Granny to parry with Grumby, and he even considers the possibility of physically holding her back.

Enough time has elapsed since the last story to allow Granny, Ringo, and Bayard to establish their "mule borrowing" activities as a highly successful operation. Granny simply uses some embossed, engraved Yankee stationery, finds a camp that has a sufficient number of mules in it for her purposes, and then rides into the camp; there, she is given the requisitioned number of mules, which she later sells back to the Yankees (keeping only what is needed for local farming). Using the money she receives, she divides it up into shares and distributes it to various needy people in the county. In this story, then, she emerges as the central character and Bayard remains essentially in the background; in the next stories, however, Bayard will resume his initial importance as the principal character in the novel.

The opening line of the story introduces us to Ab Snopes, one of Faulkner's most interesting creations. Ab is the founder of a large family which will ultimately wheedle and connive its way into every aspect of life in Yoknapatawpha County. And it is Ab Snopes who will unconsciously contribute to Granny's death because of his greed; yet it should be noted that even though Ab is basically a cowardly man, he is never as treacherous as Grumby, the unprincipled leader of a gang of renegades.

At the beginning of the story, Granny is disappointed with the amount of money that Ab received for the last bunch of mules he sold in Memphis. Money is critical; as we saw in the last story, the countryside lies in almost complete desolation, and the poor people and the blacks are in need of all the help that they can get. Even Ab Snopes alludes to this fact when he acknowledges that it would ultimately be easier for Granny to bargain for more money for the horses and mules; perhaps she could go herself and deal more shrewdly than Ab is able to. Granny, however, is beginning to be wary of the great risk that she is taking in selling and re-selling the mules so that Ab can, in turn, sell them once again. For that reason, this story opens on an ominous note, emphasizing the danger and the desperation of the survivors of the war who must try and eke out a living on the land with no crops, no equipment, no mules, no money, and very little hope. Even Bayard notices the toll that the long, difficult war is having on his grandmother: "She didn't look any thinner or any older. She didn't look sick either. She just looked like somebody that has quit sleeping at night." In contrast to Drusilla in the last story, who intentionally quit sleeping because there was too much excitement and too much to do, Granny, meanwhile, has begun to take the burden of feeding and caring for the people of the land upon her old, thin shoulders.

At the present moment, we learn that Granny has requisitioned and sold back to the Yankees about one hundred and five mules for a total of $6,725.62. They also have more than forty mules corralled in a pen that Bayard and Ringo built in a hidden niche. But everyone knows that Granny doesn't have that much money on her, and everyone likewise knows that she has shared all of the money with the poor people of the county.

After Ringo returns from his scouting trip to see where the Yankee troops are stationed, they plan their next operation, and while they are planning it, it is almost as if Bayard were no more than the objective narrator, observing the events but not participating in them. Part of this is due to the fact that since the Yankees are fighting to free the blacks, they would never suspect a young black (Ringo) of helping the southern whites; whereas if Bayard were caught, he would now, at fifteen, most likely be made a prisoner. After all, many fifteen-year-olds were fighting on the front lines of the war.

Ringo reports that a Yankee named Colonel Newberry has just arrived with nineteen head of mules, but Granny has unexplainable qualms about signing an order for these mules, especially since this particular regiment is now in the same county. But Ringo talks her out of her objections and, still using the original requisition forms that they got in Alabama from Colonel Dick, they create one more letter of requisition, signing General Smith's name to the letter, stamped with an official letterhead: UNITED STATES FORCES. DEPARTMENT OF TENNESSEE.

The procedure they use is always the same. Granny drives up to an officer's tent (this time, it is Colonel Newberry's) with the order, and they manage to arrive at exactly the right time—that is, around dark, near supper time, when the men are tired and hungry. She hands the requisition to the officer in charge and, in a few minutes, he instructs his soldiers to give the woman (whatever fictitious name Granny chooses to use at that time; this time it is Mrs. Plurella Harris) the requisitioned mules. This time, however, Granny's scheme is not successful. Ringo does manage to get the mules and give them to Ab Snopes, and Granny and Bayard do slowly ride off in the wagon, but it is not long before they are suddenly surrounded by a group of Yankees who demand to know the whereabouts of the mules; they boast they have been on the lookout for Granny for over a month. At that moment, Ringo yells from a distance and distracts the Yankees, and Granny and Bayard get out of the wagon and hide. Next morning, Ringo finds them and they all head home in a "borrowed" buggy and two horses that he has obtained somewhere during the night. This is the end of their mule-selling operation, but at least they obtained, according to Ringo, "two hundred and forty-eight head while the business lasted." Granny, however, corrects him, reminding him that they lost their team of two mules when they were cornered by the Yankees.

Throughout this first section, the emphasis is upon the clever machinations involved in deceiving the enemy. In terms of the total novel, we must remember that Granny's house—that is, the Sartoris mansion—has been destroyed by the Yankees, and the land and the countryside have been left desolate. It is because of these factors that she feels absolutely justified in taking the mules. After all, historically, the Yankees were a well-provided army, and Granny is watching out for her own folks—both white and black—who are starving in the now desolate countryside. It is not that she is, by nature, a deceptive woman. Quite the contrary; there is something innately good, something that we admire in a woman who sees woman and children and old people (white and black) dying of hunger and starvation and takes it upon herself to do something about it. Granny's code of behavior does not involve abstract principles: she sees living people in desperate need of the very basics of life, and she means to do something about it. The war is not nearly as important as is the fact that hungry human beings are dying.

In the second section of the story, Granny goes to church and offers up a prayer that—better than anything else in the novel—

characterizes her and her philosophy of life. But remember that in terms of the story, Granny doesn't exactly "pray" to God: As Ringo said in "Raid," Granny will decide "what she want and then she kneel down about ten seconds and tell God what she aim to do, and then she git up and do it." Here, in this prayer, there is a sense of Granny's telling God what she aims to do, and there is also the suggestion that she is having a kind of "running argument" with Him. After all, according to the southern point of view, it is God who "saw fit to make it [the Civil War] a lost cause." As a result, when the war ceases to be Granny's "holy cause" and becomes a lost cause, Granny herself has to take action.

Alone in the empty church, with only Bayard, Ringo, and Joby, Granny says, "I have sinned. I have stolen, and I have borne false witness against my neighbor, though that neighbor was an enemy of my country." And lest God forget, she reminds Him very firmly that she "did not sin for gain or for greed. . . . I did not sin for revenge. I defy You or anyone to say I did. I sinned first for justice." Later, she admits to having sinned for "the sake of food and clothes for Your creatures." She then informs God that if she kept back some of the things she gained, then she is "the best judge of that." Her prayer thus carries a dual tone of deep devotion and admirable defiance. She will not let God blame anyone except herself for what has happened. If there is to be punishment, then that punishment is to fall on her thin but strong shoulders. Unknowingly, this retribution will come shortly in the form of Grumby, an unprincipled and degenerate renegade.

In general terms, section three of the story begins sometime later. Apparently Ab Snopes has informed the enemy of the whereabouts of the penned-up mules, and a company of Yankee soldiers arrives to recapture them. The Yankee officer in charge tries to make a bargain with Granny and make her tell him exactly how many mules she requisitioned and how many of those she sold back to the Yankees and then requisitioned again. Granny tells him firmly that she doesn't know how many. At first, he doesn't believe her; then he begins to realize that the operation has been so totally successful that she really *doesn't* know how many mules they have trafficked in. The officer then explains that if she writes out any more requisitions, then *he* (a poor man with a family) will have to pay for the Yankee loss, and he asks her, specifically, to promise not to use his name. Granny assures him that he need not worry. After the officer has left, Ringo informs Granny that it was Ab Snopes who informed the Yankees about the mules; he says that Ab Snopes is so greedy that he can't rest until some more money is made off of all of the mules.

Section four deals with one of the major climaxes in the novel, and note that it is told somewhat in retrospect, with Bayard saying, "We tried to keep her from doing it—we both tried." That is, after Ringo told Granny about Ab Snopes, Bayard tries to keep her from doing anything about Ab's betrayal; he doesn't want her involved anymore. But Bayard still doesn't believe, even after Granny is killed, that Ab intended for her to be killed by Grumby.

Despite all of Bayard's protests, however, Granny insists on seeing the renegade desperado named Grumby, who has been living on the fears of deserted women and children, taking what few provisions there are left in the countryside. Moreover, Granny feels that because Grumby is a southerner, he would never—under any circumstance—harm an old woman, and a lady at that. But the times are changing; the war is getting worse every day, and Granny and the boys have just found out that Drusilla, who has been missing for a year, has been riding with John Sartoris's troops as though she were a man herself. This fact in itself brings the reality of the war's metamorphosis into terms which the boys can understand.

If John Sartoris can ride about the country protecting women and children, then Granny cannot envision another southerner, such as Grumby and his fifty or sixty men, being anything less than honorable to his fellow southerners. Yet whereas Colonel Sartoris is fighting the Yankees wherever he can find them, Grumby never enters an area until he is sure that all of the Yankees have gone; then he ravages the countryside. Some time ago, Grumby was captured, but he managed to produce some type of document which was purportedly signed by a General Forrest, appointing him a commissioned raider against the rebels. The men who captured him, however, were old men, and they did not have the strength or wits to hold him. Now he rides through the night, creating terror among the already frightened and hungry whites and blacks.

Ab Snopes, somehow, has discovered—"how Ab Snopes knew it he didn't say"—that Granny could get at least two thousand dollars if she would sign *one* more order—this time for some thoroughbred horses, and Ab promises Granny that she can get two thousand dollars out of Grumby. Granny, who has taken care of almost everyone else in the country, suddenly realizes that very soon her son-in-law (Colonel Sartoris) will be coming home to a ruined planta- tion, and she decides to try to get him some fifteen hundred dollars in cash (Ab Snopes, of course, will want to keep one of the mares as his commission, leaving only fifteen hundred dollars from the two thousand dollars which Ab thinks will be profit).

Bayard begs Granny to seek advice from Uncle Buck McCaslin, or anyone else; he knows, even at his young age, that a person can make a bargain with a brave man, but Grumby is a coward and, worse than that, Grumby is a frightened coward; these two facts make him the most dangerous type of man possible for Granny to deal with. But Granny doesn't listen to Bayard, so Ab takes her to Grumby's hiding place on the Tallahatchie River, the border of Yoknapatawpha County. Granny, furthermore, will not allow Bayard and Ringo to go with her to Grumby's camp because they both look like grown men now, and they might be hurt. But she is confident that Grumby and his men will not hurt her since she is an old woman and, in addition, she is an elderly southern lady. Bayard threatens to hold her back because he is stronger than she is, but, after all these years of obeying Granny, he can't suddenly physically restrain her; his deep love and respect for her will not allow it. Gran- ny firmly maintains: "I am taking no risk; I am a woman. Even Yankees do not harm old women." Of course, Granny's mistake is that she assumes that Grumby is a decent person. While it is true that even Yankees don't hurt old women, Grumby is a different breed of person, one who has no respect for the North or for the South or for women or for children—of any race.

When Ringo sees Grumby and his band of men leave, he and Bayard run to the old compress (a building used for baling cotton). There, in the faint light of the afternoon, they see Granny's small dead body. Earlier she had looked "little alive, but now she looked like she had collapsed, like she had been made out of a lot of little thin dry light sticks . . . and all the little sticks had collapsed in a quiet heap on the floor, and somebody had spread a clean and fad- ed calico dress over them." With the horrible, appalling death of Granny, Bayard is faced with his most momentous task—avenging her death against a known renegade murderer, one who would bush-whack and kill Bayard without the slightest compunction.

Granny dies, then, in the service of other people. Her final act is one that would have given her son-in-law, Colonel Sartoris, and her other relatives some money to start all over again after the fighting was over. Faulkner, or Bayard, never mentions the idea, but they both seem to tacitly accept the fact that the great "lost cause" is now in its final stages, and that it is only a matter of a very short time before the South's fall and subsequent restoration (the Reconstruction) begins. Looking back, it is significant to note that during most of Miss Rosa's—or Granny's—actions, she was very severe with herself. Of course, however, she was severe with others too. When she comically insisted on having the boys' mouths wash-ed out with soap in the first story because they uttered a curse word, she was equally severe later when she judged herself and her own ac-tions. But these are hard times and Granny has had to adhere to her principles more firmly than she has ever done before. Never before has she been forced to consider her basic principles and never before has she been forced to act on them, but now her principles require that she deal with the war-torn realities of her land with acts of kind-ness and love for other human beings—whether they happen to be the lost black mother in "Raid," or whether they happen to be the country folks in this particular story who need mules in order to cultivate their meager plots of ground. In short, Granny's philosophy and her religion concern themselves with the perfor-mance of good deeds. No intellectual schema is needed for what she feels must be done in these times.

VENDÉE

This story moves faster than any of the other stories in the novel, possibly because Faulkner does not let anything get in Bayard's way of revenging his grandmother's murder. All of the single parts of the story move toward his tracking down Grumby and, then, exhibiting the murderer's remains—nailing his corpse to the door of the compress like a coon hide. In addition, the organiza-tion of this story is also the most compact of all the stories in the novel. Basically, it is divided into four parts: part one deals with

Granny's (Miss Rosa's) funeral; part two involves the tracking down and thrashing of Ab Snopes for his part in Granny's death; part three concerns Bayard's tracking down and killing Grumby, thus bringing about the culmination of the revenge; and part four very briefly tells of the boys' homecoming and how they disposed of Grumby's body and hung his right hand from a cross above Granny's grave.

Like the title of the other stories in this novel, this one is interesting in itself, having a double meaning. First, "Vendée" could refer to the town in France which was the scene of a Royalist revolt during the French Revolution. But the actions of the Royalists, revolting against the predominant commoners who were in charge of the revolution, would be an ironic reversal in this story since Grumby, the lowest scum on any social scale, is using the chaos at the end of the Civil War as an excuse to ravage, pillage, and terrorize the surviving southerners—mostly women, children, and blacks. The second meaning of "vendée" refers to a person to whom something has been sold—or to a buyer. In the last story, had things worked according to Granny's plan, Grumby would have been a "vendée" (or seller, of sorts). Granny went to Grumby in good faith to make an ambiguous, illegal deal concerning some thoroughbred horses, thinking that he was a gentleman of his word and would honor an old woman's request simply because she was old and a southern lady. She hoped to realize about fifteen hundred dollars from the deal (Ab Snopes would have kept one of Grumby's mares, worth about five hundred dollars). Of course, Faulkner's title could also, possibly, refer to the fact that Bayard and Ringo are going to hunt Grumby down and "sell him a bill of goods" he didn't ask for—his own death.

Bayard's feeling that he *must* avenge Granny's murder is seen most clearly during the funeral scene. Note the people who come to her funeral: besides the friends of the family, and those from Jefferson, remember that also present are the twelve blacks she feels particularly responsible for, plus the hundred or so blacks from the hills who have returned and live in caves and hollow trees. It is these people whom Granny felt responsible for and whom she cared for and fed and shared what money she made. She provided these people with mules and money to keep them alive; in fact, almost everyone in the county is indebted to Granny in some way or another. Note, too, that many of the country people ride in on mules that have long black smears on their hips where Ringo and Granny "had burned out the U.S. brand."

In the midst of all this dramatic seriousness, however, Faulkner inserts a masterful, light comic touch. Granny's closest friend from town, Mrs. Compson, has arranged for a prestigious preacher to come all the way from Memphis to conduct Granny's funeral, and one of Mrs. Compson's blacks is holding an umbrella over this important preacher's head; suddenly in the midst of this rain-soaked ceremony which is about to begin, Brother Fortinbride (who isn't even a minister, who was just a private in Colonel Sartoris' regiment and miraculously survived a seemingly fatal wound) takes over the ceremony. His ministering to the hill folks just "sprang right up out of the ground," Bayard says. Brother Fortinbride doesn't object to the fancy preacher who has been "refugeed in" from Memphis; he just knows how Granny would have wanted things done: it is raining and the hill folks need to get home, and so they bury Granny, with old Uncle Buck helping, his rheumatism so bad he won't be able to move shortly, but doing as much shoveling as anyone else. Then Brother Fortinbride delivers the type of funeral message that Granny would have approved of: "I don't reckon that anybody that ever knew her would want to insult her by telling her to rest anywhere in peace. And I reckon that God has already seen to it that there are men, women, and children, black, white, yellow or red, waiting for her to tend and worry over. And so you folks go home. . . . You have wood to cut and split. . . . and what do you reckon Rosa Millard would say about you all standing around here, keeping old folks and children out here in the rain?" This funeral oration brings to a close Miss Rosa's active participation in the events of the story, yet her presence will be felt throughout the remainder of the story because of Bayard's deep need to avenge her murder.

Mrs. Compson and some of the others invite Bayard (and Ringo, of course) to come live with them, but these people do not understand the immensity of the task that Bayard feels that he must accomplish. Uncle Buck McCaslin, however, understands exactly what Bayard feels, and he has a good idea what Bayard and Ringo are planning to do. He also knows that they don't have a gun and that he does have a weapon suitable for tracking down Grumby.

Seriously, yet ultimately humorously, Ringo suggests that they use the half-burnt barrel of Colonel Sartoris's musket; that would be good enough, he says, to track down Ab Snopes—since Ab is a coward and not much more than half a man, anyway. Yet, significantly, this comment of Ringo's is the first indication in the entire novel that Ringo isn't nearly as perceptive as Bayard is. In the earlier stories, when they were all involved in the mule swapping, it was, more often than not, Ringo who was the shrewder and the more clever of the two in any situation. Here, however, Ringo assumes that it was Ab Snopes—not Grumby—who was responsible for Granny's death. Bayard, however, knows that Ab Snopes was just an insignificant pawn to the evil, degenerate Grumby.

The three of them decide to go after Grumby, but they decide first to find Ab Snopes because he will lead them to Grumby, and second, Ab must be punished for his part in Granny's death. As they approach Ab's cabin, they come upon a pen holding a claybank (yellow) stallion and three mares (Grumby's horses). Uncle Buck tells the boys that this is a ruse; Grumby hid the horses there to throw them off the track if they managed to find Ab's cabin. He then asks Bayard and Ringo to stay back while he inquires about Ab's whereabouts; he is sure that Ab will be with Grumby and his men. A woman peers out of the cabin and tells Uncle Buck that Ab has gone to Alabama, but Uncle Buck is sure that Grumby has gone in another direction, anywhere but toward Alabama.

The first part of the story, then, sets the revenge machinery in motion. Bayard, Uncle Buck, and Ringo know that Grumby will be constantly on the move and that Ab Snopes will be with them; furthermore, they can track Grumby and his men because wherever they find the remains of pillaging, or hear of pillaging, they can be sure that Grumby is not far ahead.

In theory, it should be realized that the act of revenging Granny's death should be done by Colonel Sartoris; he, however, has assembled a company of irregulars. In other words, Colonel Sartoris is not stationed with, or assigned to, any recognized southern battalion; therefore, since he is his own commander, only he himself decides where he will go to attack the Yankees. It is impossible, then, to contact him. He could be anywhere. As a consequence, the act of revenge falls to Granny's fifteen- (almost sixteen) year-old grandson. Also, too, this is during a time of stress and conflict and, at this point during the war, historically, there were many fifteen-year-old boys fighting on the front lines; therefore, while Bayard's acts seem almost overly mature today, when men are not drafted until they are eighteen, in terms of what Bayard has witnessed and what he has undergone concerning the Civil War, he is mature well beyond his fifteen, almost sixteen, years.

In part two, the relentless pursuit of Grumby begins. It will last from December until sometime in February; the exact time is not certain because Ringo has to use the stick that he's been keeping notches in to keep track of the days in order to start a fire and warm Uncle Buck's arthritic arm. Meanwhile, regiments of hill people volunteer their services to help track down Grumby, but Grumby is not easy to follow because of his violent, non-stop ravaging and raping of the countryside. "Kill them. Kill them" are cries that the three hear wherever they go, referring to the fact that Grumby has already been there and is just ahead of them. They can't keep pace with his path of destruction. Here, Faulkner is creating a picture of a man who is so barbaric and so inhuman that Bayard's own savage act at the story's conclusion will be applauded rather than disapproved of.

Ringo locates the band of outlaws one day, but Grumby and his men escape; yet the three realize that they are now so close to Grumby that they can now follow the horses' hoof prints. Later, while they are eating, a stranger with a hat and a beard so black and big that only his eyes show, rides up and joins them. He says that he is riding toward Alabama looking for a man named Grumby who killed one of the man's slaves and ran his horses off. He wonders if Uncle Buck and the boys are looking for the same person. Ringo, despite Uncle Buck's hushing, offers the information that they are looking for two: "Two is correct. . . . I reckon Ab Snopes can pass for a man."

Ringo's comment here, while humorous, is consistent with his characterization throughout the rest of the stories—that is, he often speaks without thinking. In this case, reticence is called for. Uncle Buck and Bayard are pretty sure that this man is either Grumby himself or else someone that Grumby has sent out as a decoy to get information. In this case of doubt, reticence is better than revealing the truth, but Ringo is always one to speak whatever is on his mind.

When the stranger starts to leave, he warns them to forget about Grumby, to confine their search to Ab Snopes. He then mounts up and, while doing so, fires a shot into the group, wounding Uncle Buck in the underside of his arthritic arm. As the stranger gallops off, Ringo, more observant here than the others, notices that one of the stranger's horse's back shoes is missing. It is not until later in the story that we find out that this man is *not* Grumby himself; this man is merely a member of Grumby's band. But apparently the stranger thinks that his warning to confine their search to Ab Snopes, in addition to his pistol shot into the group, wounding Uncle Buck, will be enough to persuade them not to trail Grumby any farther. Yet the three continue on, and they find Ab Snopes, tied up and hitched to a sapling. Obviously Grumby hopes that when Bayard, Ringo, and Uncle Buck find Snopes, their desire for revenge will be satisfied; furthermore, Grumby probably also hopes that because of Uncle Buck's wound, that they will turn back. He is wrong. Ringo notices an unshod hoof print in the dirt; obviously, it belongs to one of the five horses that have just ridden away; thus the association between the stranger, Ab Snopes, and Grumby is now perfectly clear.

When they untie Snopes, he begins immediately to holler and scream about how they "caught and robbed him, and they would have killed him if they hadn't heard [someone] coming and run away." Bayard, however, observes that Snopes's "eyes were not hollering." Bayard has begun to tell a man's character by watching his eyes; he knows that Ab Snopes is lying.

When Ab Snopes will say nothing about Grumby, Bayard is ready to fight him, but Snopes falls to the ground, whining that there are three of them against one of him. When Ringo tries to pick Snopes up, Snopes keeps falling back to the ground, so they tie him to a tree and Bayard thrashes him with a whip made out of galluses and bridle reins. But Snopes says nothing; he knows that if he says anything, Grumby's men will find out about it and will come back and kill him. He also feels that as much as Bayard might beat him, ultimately Bayard will not kill him.

Note here and also in the final story ("An Odor of Verbena") that Ringo, because he is black, is allowed to participate only so much in this matter of revenge. As he is about to approach Ab Snopes to take part in the revenge, Uncle Buck orders Ringo to "stay back." Even though Ab Snopes belongs to the lowest class of white people, in terms of "the old order" of the South, a black man cannot raise his hand to a white person—however guilty or evil that white person might be, or however good the black man might be. But Ringo's astuteness concerning the missing horseshoe contributes to the revenge, so he does manage to take part in the final retribution of Granny's murder. The marks of the unshod hoof will make identification certain that the stranger, Snopes, and Grumby are part of the same band. Now, however, because Uncle Buck's wound is becoming increasingly more painful, he must turn back; this he does, taking Snopes with him. Bayard and Ringo are alone, on their own to find Grumby.

Whereas part two covered Uncle Buck's and Bayard's (and, in a sense, Ringo's) revenge against Ab Snopes, part three will concern itself with the final revenge exacted against Grumby, who knows that he is being pursued. This is evident when Bayard and Ringo find a note, warning them to turn back. Then they find a second note, written in a very fine script and in a highly polished style, offering them a chance to live if they turn back now; it is apparent that the second note is written by the mysterious stranger who possesses the dainty hands, "with a light mat of fine black hair right down to the finger nails."

The next day, this bearded stranger steps out of some bushes with a pistol aimed directly at Bayard and Ringo. Another man is with him, leading a third man—"a thick-built man with a reddish stubble and pale eyes, in a faded Confederate uniform coat and Yankee boots, bare-headed, with a long smear of dried blood on his cheek. . . . and then all of a sudden we knew that at last we were looking at Grumby." The bearded man, Matt Bowden, has Grumby tied up, but, surprisingly, he cuts Grumby loose, throws a gun at his feet, and tells Grumby how he ruined things for them because one day "you lost your nerve and killed an old woman and then lost your nerve again and refused to cover the first mistake." As the two men turn to ride away, Grumby grabs the gun from the ground and fires three shots after them.

Grumby then tries to convince Bayard and Ringo that he has no more bullets in his gun. Bayard knows better. Then Bayard tells us that he isn't quite sure what happened next: two bright orange splashes appeared against the middle of Grumby's Confederate coat, then Bayard "reckon[s] he heard the sound . . . heard the bullets . . . reckon I felt him when he hit me, but *I don't remember it*" (emphasis mine). Bayard does, however, remember seeing

Grumby on top of him and Ringo astraddle of Grumby, "his open pocket knife in his hand." At first, Bayard is unable to raise his arm, but when Grumby bucks Ringo off his back and begins to run, Bayard is at last able to raise his arm toward Grumby's back and "the pistol was level and steady as a rock."

Perhaps it should be pointed out here that Ringo's being astraddle Grumby does not violate the code of the South, concerning a black man's place on the social scale. Earlier, Ringo was not allowed to take out his anger on Ab Snopes; then, however, there were two white men who were able to deal with another white man, Snopes. Here, the situation is very different. Bayard's life is threatened, and Ringo must act to save this young white man who has been as close as a brother to him. There is no violation of the southern code; Ringo is saving Bayard's life when Bayard can no longer save himself.

The third section of the story ends, and Faulkner leaves us with the assumption that Bayard has shot Grumby. He does not, however, dwell on the violence of the revenge; instead, Faulkner deals primarily with the causes and the justifications for the revenge. And here, he uses Bayard's narration in an interesting fictional technique: Bayard is narrating a scene where confusion reigns; he hears shots, he is unable to move, Grumby is on top of him, and, most important, he is *not sure* what happened. We have a sense of sudden violence occurring, but Faulkner does not tell us exactly what happened and the effect is far more dazzling than had he recounted actual facts and details.

In section four, some time has passed, and as is traditional in most of Faulkner's fiction, he does not dwell on the "gruesome" acts that the boys feel that they have to perform. When the section opens, these acts are already over with, and the boys are on their way to Granny's grave, carrying something lightweight, wrapped in the tail of Grumby's coat. At her grave, they find that someone has put up a type of marker, so all they have to do is remove the object from their package and wire it to the temporary grave marker, with Ringo's pronouncement, "Now she can lay good and quiet." Then the boys cry for the first time, and Ringo astutely points out that, "it wasn't him [Grumby] or Ab Snopes either that kilt her. . . . It was them mules. That first batch of mules we got for nothing."

Arriving home, Bayard and Ringo find out that the war is over and that Colonel Sartoris and Drusilla have been home for a week and have been out looking for them, led by Uncle Buck. The boys fall asleep, despite the good news, but are awakened sometime later by Colonel Sartoris and Drusilla and by the yelling of Uncle Buck, announcing to all the whites and all the blacks—and everyone else who can possibly hear him—exactly what Bayard has done. Drusilla tries to hush Uncle Buck, but he is determined to tell the whole story. Not only was Grumby tracked down, but the "murdering scoundrel" was nailed to the door of the old compress, "all except the right hand," and if anyone wants to know where that is, they can go "look on Rosa Millard's grave." Uncle Buck then confirms that Bayard is indeed "John Sartoris' boy."

This section once again shows Faulkner's fictional technique of withholding information. The events are not told in chronological order. In fact, we don't know what Bayard had wrapped in the tail of Grumby's coat that is so lightweight; we don't know until the last line of the story, when it is finally made clear that the hand that shot and killed Granny now hangs above her grave as "proof and expiation" that revenge is complete; now she can rest in peace. This is a bloosy act, and even Drusilla, a woman given to violence normally, tries to hush the narrating of it. Furthermore, not even Faulkner tells us what happened to Grumby's body; he has Uncle Buck tell about its being nailed to the old compress, where Grumby murdered Granny.

The news that the war is over now explains why the bearded stranger handed Grumby over to Bayard and Ringo. Since the war is over and the men will be returning home, had Grumby *not* been killed, all of the returning southern soldiers would have rounded up enough men to hunt down and kill every person in Grumby's band. By yielding up Grumby himself, the stranger with the black beard and the others feel that perhaps they are free to escape toward Texas without being followed because Grumby was the one directly associated with all of the barbaric acts committed against all the poor, defenseless southern women and children.

The story ends at the same time that the Civil War is ending. The trials faced by the Sartoris clan will now differ significantly due to the changing times in the now-defeated South.

SKIRMISH AT SARTORIS

In terms of the entire novel, this story concerns itself with the rapid social changes that took place in the South immediately following the Civil War. Bayard is still the narrator of the story, but here he is not the focus of the story's actions; he is more of an outside observer. Likewise, Ringo, who has figured prominently in all the stories, has virtually no role in this story. In "Skirmish," the main conflict has a double focus, each of almost equal importance. The title suggests that there is only *one* skirmish, but there are two skirmishes—first, the political skirmish involving the Missouri carpetbaggers' attempts to insure that the Negroes of Jefferson exercise their right to vote for Marshal. The more important skirmish, however, involves Aunt Louisa's attempts to get John Sartoris and Drusilla Hawk married. This last "skirmish" seems as though it was a comical (superficial or tongue-in-cheek) sub-plot, but in reality, the basis of any civilization depends upon strict adherence to certain social norms; marriage and the family is the basis of civilization, and any threat to that social unit is most serious. Yet Faulkner treats the carpetbagger theme far more seriously, and he treats the marriage theme in a much lighter, more humorous manner. In fact, the subject of the right to vote is treated with, literally, dead seriousness. The right for some people to vote and the denial of that right for other people is a perversion of justice, and it is this theme which more seriously undermines and destroys the primary concepts of society, upon which the first theme elaborates. In other words, if in the process of restricting voting rights, we destroy the basic foundation (the family) of society, there would be no need to vote for anything.

The structure of southern civilization has been almost totally destroyed; its houses and mansions have been burned (see "Retreat" and "Raid"), its railroads destroyed (see "Retreat"), its economy destroyed, its women and children murdered or homeless, its morale shattered, and its political, social, and philosophical premises are now being put to their most severe test: will the surviving southern gentry, who fought to preserve a system built on slavery allow the northern carpetbaggers to organize the Negroes and make them exercise their newly decreed right to vote as free citizens? Democracy hinges upon the right of all its citizens to participate in the electoral process; in the Civil War just ended, the North fought to uphold these principles. Yet here, even after the war is over, the skirmish continues, albeit on a smaller scale: will the Negroes—now free and recognized as citizens—still be denied their rights?

Consequently, the story asks what is more important—the right to vote or the reestablishment of a *normal* society, based upon the family as the basic unit of that society? For example, how important is the right to vote when the family as a unit no longer exists? Seen in this context, Faulkner's comic theme, treated humorously, seriously concerns the very basis of any civilized society. Both the right of adults to marry whomever they choose and the right of adults to vote for whomever they choose should be inalienable rights of any society; yet in this story, set in a devastated, almost destroyed society, both inalienable rights are perverted.

In terms of Faulkner's structure, the story has three basic divisions—each one emphasizing both themes ("skirmishes"). The opening sentence presents the basic confrontation both between the matter of the marriage and the matter of the voting: "When I think of that day, of Father's old troop on their horses drawn up facing the house, and Father and Drusilla on the ground with the carpetbagger voting box in front of them, and opposite them the women—Aunt Louisa, Mrs. Habersham and all the others—on the porch and the two sets of them, the men and the women, facing one another like they were both waiting for a bugle to sound the charge, I think I know the reason." After this long opening sentence, one is inclined to think that the "skirmish" of the title is going to be between the men and the women squared off and facing one another. But this is Faulkner's way of creating suspense and interest, and he is successful. After we have witnessed the unity of the men and the women in the previous stories, this sentence is startling. Faulkner needed this ploy; "Vendée" realized and resolved a major crisis. Now Faulkner must continue his novel, and he needs a sufficient "hook" to keep his readers reading about the aftermath of the war. We keep reading, watching him use this first sentence to enlarge his ideas and create three sections in this story which combine both of his themes. In this sense, "Skirmish" is as unified a story as "Ambuscade" or "Vendée."

In this particular story, however, the *function* of the narrator, as opposed to the *role* of the narrator, changes. Here, Bayard is treated by the adults as being very immature and in need of moral protection—a view that is certainly not warranted after all he has done, dealt with, and had to make decisions about. In each of the earlier stories, Bayard worked alongside older men, and in "Vendée," he performed an act of revenge requiring fortitude and endurance far beyond the capabilities of most fifteen-year-old boys; here, we realized that he was no longer a mere boy. Likewise, as narrator of this particular story, Bayard demonstrates mature insights into social situations that far exceed his chronological fifteen years. Yet one of the concerns of the "ladies" in this story is that Drusilla's and John Sartoris's not marrying might have a corruptive influence on this fifteen-year-old. Ironically, Bayard remains largely unaffected, serving as Faulkner's uninvolved narrator, one who reports only the action of the story.

In this first section, it is suggested that (according to the women) since the men "had given in and admitted that they belonged to the United States," they proved that they lacked a solid moral code; they might do anything now. Their admitting that they belong once more to the United States might prelude any kind of immoral, unnatural behavior. In contrast to the men of the South, "the women had never surrendered." To them, marriage *was* important and it still *is* important. As soldiers of a sort together, Drusilla and John rode together, fought together, and the ladies assume, probably had sex together; thus they must be married.

Drusilla, remember, asked Bayard in "Raid" to ask Bayard's father if she could ride with Colonel Sartoris's troops. Now, we read that she did, in fact, accomplish that goal; she has been fighting with John's troops for almost a year; and, of course, at the end of "Vendeé," Faulkner included a short scene in which she and John returned to the ruins of the Sartoris plantation.

Bayard and Ringo are still fifteen, as we noted, when this story begins. A letter from Hawkhurst, Alabama, arrives and reminds Bayard of that night long ago (actually only eighteen months ago) when Drusilla first expressed her wish to join Colonel Sartoris's troops. But Bayard forgot to mention it to his father; yet, Drusilla was so determined that she found Colonel Sartoris himself and rode with him and his troops anyway. To Aunt Louisa, Drusilla deliberately tried to "unsex herself" because Drusilla refused to show any grief over the death of her father or her fiancé (Gavin Breckbridge) in the traditional way—that is, weeping and wailing and wearing black. Instead, Drusilla saddled up and rode off to the front lines and confronted and fought the Yankees who killed her men folks.

Then another letter arrives, addressed to Miss Rosa (Granny), beginning "Dear Sister." Granny, of course, is now dead, but it is the contents which are of central concern here. In the letter, Aunt Louisa is obviously grieved that Drusilla's father died trying to protect the sanctity of southern womanhood, an ideal which Drusilla is now flagrantly violating. In the letter, Aunt Louisa laments to her sister about Mr. Hawk, who "laid down his life to protect a heritage of . . . spotless women." Aunt Louisa is not content with mere letter writing; however; she activates her "army"—the women of Jefferson and Yoknapatawpha County—who mean to see to it that a marriage takes place between Colonel Sartoris and Drusilla, who "had been reserved for . . . the highest destiny of a Southern women—to be the bride-widow of a lost cause" has now become a "lost woman and a shame" because not only did Drusilla ride with Sartoris's men, she bivouacked with them, whacked off her hair, and, most dreadful of all, wore a man's uniform—and not just a man's uniform, but that of *a common private soldier.*

Drusilla strongly opposes and rejects these traditional southern views about womanhood and about herself. When Aunt Louisa insists that her daughter and John get married, Drusilla explains, "Can't you understand that I am tired of burying husbands in this war? That I am riding in Cousin John's troop not to find a man but to hurt Yankees?"

In section two, it is spring; the war is over, Faulkner reminds us again, and Drusilla has once again donned men's clothes, and she is working out in the fields, just like another man. Ringo, who previously shared a pallet with Bayard in one of the former slave quarters, has moved to the cabin where Joby and Louvinia live, and now Bayard and Colonel Sartoris sleep on a pallet in the cabin, and Drusilla sleeps in a bed behind a quilt that has been tacked up to divide the cabin into two sleeping quarters. That spring, Mrs. Compson, who does not even know Aunt Louisa Hawk, receives a letter, addressed to her this time, from Aunt Louisa, emphasizing the fact that "the good name of one family was the good name of all." This key comment brings us back to the main theme—that is, in a period of flux, change, and reconstruction, the survival of the institution of marriage and the family is essential to the survival of society as a whole. With this theme in mind, remember that despite the reason for the war itself, and despite the fact that the war is over the whites still separate themselves from the blacks at the Sartoris plantation. For example, Ringo no longer sleeps with Bayard, as he did for fifteen years; instead, Ringo is now sent to sleep with Joby and Louvinia. This suggests the beginning of serious segregation once again, and here the balloting for Marshal of Jefferson is a matter which will become the climax of the social theme.

The "skirmish" at Sartoris, referred to in the title, begins when Mrs. Habersham, who does not even know Drusilla, brings a number of ladies out from town to the Sartoris plantation to see for themselves what is going on. There is a total of fourteen women, and their main concern is to determine the exact nature of the sleeping arrangements. Bayard tells us, "It was Mrs. Habersham who was holding back the quilt for the others to go in and look at the bed where Drusilla slept and then showing them the pallet where Father and I slept." Bayard overhears the gossip of the ladies, but he ignores it, especially when the ladies keep obsequiously referring to Bayard as "you poor child." We must remember that Bayard, in the last story ("Vendée"), performed a murder and nailed a man's corpse to a door—more than enough for him to be classified as an adult—and certainly not as a "poor child," even though this story does repeatedly emphasize that he is *only* fifteen years old. (Actually, in terms of the entire novel, Bayard is presented fictionally as younger and more immature in this story than in the last, but originally, each of these stories—except "An Odor of Verbena"—was published separately in magazines.)

When the fourteen ladies approach Drusilla about her "condition," as they call it, she doesn't understand what they mean at first. When it finally becomes clear what the ladies are implying—that she is living at the Sartoris house to sleep with John Sartoris, or is now sleeping with him, or else intends to compromise him into a position where he will be *forced* to marry her—Drusilla is both horrified and distraught. She immediately asks the colonel, " 'John, John. . . . Is that what you think too?' she said. Then she was gone." To Louvinia, who holds Drusilla comfortingly, Drusilla sobs that she and John "went to the war to hurt Yankees, not hunting women!" In this statement, she ironically forgets that she *is* a woman; Drusilla's whole frame of mind—her comments about the war, on rebuilding and reconstruction, and on voting rights—is as "man-like" as are all of her previous actions. To Drusilla, what she

58

has done is innocent and morally right; to the other southern women, however, her actions have been and continue to be perverted and unnatural.

But those were strange times. Even Bayard is perplexed. For four years, they fought to get the Yankees out of the South; now, suddenly, even the most stalwart of the southern men, Colonel Sartoris himself, is counting on President Lincoln to keep his promise and "send us troops." His trust is now with a man from the North who promises to send out troops to keep out the carpetbaggers and restore order to the South. Once more, Faulkner's two themes merge again and here, on the Sartoris porch, we realize that the social order cannot be restored until Drusilla and John are married.

Ironically, the cause of the major political dissent is announced by a Negro, by Ringo. Another Negro, Cassius Q. Benbow—if the carpetbaggers are successful—is going to be elected Marshal of Jefferson. Two carpetbaggers from Missouri, named Burden, are organizing the Negroes into a single voting bloc. (For a full and complete history of the Burden family, one should read Faulkner's novel *Light in August*, in which Joanna Burden tells her view of Colonel Sartoris's murdering of her half-brother and her grandfather and how her own father retrieved the dead bodies and buried them in a hidden grave for fear that other racists might find them and desecrate the graves and the bodies.)

During these times, Colonel Sartoris is seldom at the Sartoris mansion; he and the other white men are busy rebuilding Jefferson. He is gone, for example, when Aunt Louisa arrives one day bringing trunks filled with Drusilla's dresses. The trunks contain "dresses in them that she hadn't worn in three years; Ringo never had seen her in a dress until Aunt Louisa came." (This last statement isn't actually true in terms of the entire novel; in "Raid," Ringo saw Drusilla in a dress when they were in Alabama.) This minor error on Faulkner's part is unimportant, however, in terms of the impact of Aunt Louisa's arriving with the trunks of dresses. Faulkner has Bayard say, concerning the dresses and the trunks, "Drusilla was beaten, like as soon as she let them put the dress on her she was whipped; like in the dress she could neither fight back nor run away." According to Bayard, "that's what beat Drusilla: the trunks."

Drusilla does make an attempt to convince her mother that nothing immoral occurred between her and John while they were fighting the Yankees, but Aunt Louisa will not listen, and she confronts John Sartoris directly: "Colonel Sartoris . . . I am a woman; I must request what the husband whom I have lost and the man son which I have not would demand, perhaps at the point of a pistol.—Will you marry my daughter?" Colonel Sartoris, a defeated man who has had to cope with the loss of the South, understands: to Drusilla, he says simply, "They have beat you, Drusilla." Thus the restoration of the social order is initiated.

In the background of this episode, however, looms the other theme of the story: the election of the Marshal of Jefferson. Earlier, Colonel Sartoris told the carpetbagger Burdens that the election would never be held with "Cash Benbow or any other nigger in it." Stubbornly, because they have legal authority and power and ideals, the Burdens decide to defy Colonel Sartoris and hold the election anyway.

Section three juxtaposes the two skirmishes. Aunt Louisa, totally unaware of the election, sets the date for the wedding day to be on the very day that the Marshal of Jefferson will be decided—a day when all of the men in the county would be riding to town to vote. Aunt Louisa and Mrs. Habersham, after first deciding on a big wedding for John and Drusilla, then realize that it would not be proper; so they compromise on a small, civil wedding and a big reception afterward, after Drusilla quietly meets Colonel Sartoris in town for the ceremony. On the scheduled day, people begin arriving with baskets of food and drink, and everything is prepared for the reception when Ringo and Denny suddenly ride up with the news that Drusilla and John have killed the two Burdens. Aunt Louisa's first, horrified response is not about the murders, but that Drusilla is still unmarried: "Do you mean to tell me that Drusilla and that man are not married yet?" she asks. Her first concern is not about the murder, nor even about who did it, nor even about the guilt and the implications and the possible punishment or imprisonment. Instead, Louisa's concern is only that the old social order of the South has not yet been restored: John ("that man" she calls him) and Drusilla are not yet married.

From a fictional point of view, some readers might be interested in noting that the above scene, while narrated by Bayard, is the only scene in the novel where he is not actually present. His narration relies upon Ringo and Denny's later narration of the events to him. Yet this is not as important in Faulkner's technique as is his next device. Typical of his narrative techniques in this novel, after announcing the deaths of the two Burdens, he goes back in time and narrates the events leading up to the murder. Colonel Sartoris arrived in town and saw that the voting was about to begin at the hotel. He immediately entered the hotel, followed by Drusilla, who broke through a line of men to join him. Bayard also tries to break through, but he is held back. Then they hear three shots from inside the hotel. The last two are from Colonel Sartoris's derringer. Drusilla emerges first, carrying the ballot box, the "wedding wreath on one side of her head and the veil twisted about her arm." Then Colonel Sartoris comes out, and he reminds everyone that the Burdens fired first. He appoints Drusilla Hawk as voting commissioner and announces that he will go to the sheriff and make bond because "we are working for peace through law and order." This is yet another instance of the double standard that has informed so many of the stories in this novel. Colonel Sartoris is indeed working for law and order, *but* it is a law and order based on "the old social order" of the South. His law and order involves retaining the principles under which he has always functioned and believed in and fought for. From his point of view, his land, his heritage, and his way of life—all these are sacred. For two uninvited foreigners from Missouri, two carpetbaggers, to come into Jefferson and invade the town and intrude upon a homogenized land and attempt to force, coerce, and ramrod down the throats of the people an idea and a concept that is a complete anathema to the country—this is a complete violation of the integrity of the land and its people. The land and the customs of Jefferson and of the South are still sacred, even though the war is over, and if law and order are to be the rule of the day, such violations as the Burdens advocated have to be forcibly resisted. There will be no foreign intrusion upon the sanctity of an honored homeland, especially when that land is gasping for its very existence.

The two major themes of the novel are once again united by having the ballot box being borne by Drusilla. As Colonel Sartoris says, "I reckon women don't ever surrender: not only victory, but not even defeat." Aunt Louisa, for example, is not at all concerned with the invasion of the carpetbaggers or with the voting rights of blacks; on the contrary, she deprecates the entire matter and asks of the men accompanying Drusilla: "And who are they, pray? . . . Your groomsmen of murder and robbery?" To her, the episode in town was devoid of meaning, a diversion by a man and by a woman who acts like a man. She then snatches up the polling box and throws it away. This dramatic gesture underlines an essential element of the story—that is, marriage is an honorable institution; murdering people to keep them from voting is not nearly as honorable—at least to Louisa and to the other women gathered on the porch.

Aunt Louisa wants to send immediately for the minister, but Drusilla holds out one minute longer in order to conduct the election. Earlier, the intended wedding turned into a travesty; here, the voting is certainly a travesty. One person, George Wyatt, writes out all the votes and it is announced that the outcome is unanimous: everyone voted against Benbow. As the men start the ride back to town, there is a shout of approval: "Yaaaaay, Drusilla" . . . "Yaaaaaay, John Sartoris."

In conclusion, the important skirmish of this story (the marriage of John and Drusilla) ends in defeat; the other, the skirmish involving the murder of the Burdens, and the capture of the ballot box, ends in success. Also, whereas earlier Ringo played a role as important as any white character or sometimes even more important, here, in this story dealing with the denial of voting rights to Negroes as its focal point, Ringo is virtually missing from all of the events that take place.

AN ODOR OF VERBENA

This is the only story to appear for the first time in the printed novel; that is, the first six stories originally appeared in magazines. Yet in general, critical terms, this is often considered to be the finest story in the novel.

The story involves a test. One of the oldest themes or subjects of literature involves the testing of a person's manhood. In "Vendeé," Bayard's manhood was tested in terms of his successfully tracking down Grumby and avenging his grandmother's murder. Now he is faced with another, even more severe test—one against "which I had no yardstick to measure . . . and fear [was] the test of it." Bayard will now be confronted with a greater test of his courage than was involved in the barbaric act of avenging the murder of Granny. He will be called upon to confront his own father's murderer, knowing full well his father's dictum that he *"who lives by the sword shall die by it."* This expression, or variations on this expression, are frequent throughout the story. The concept of avenging, but *not* by the sword, will be Bayard's greatest test, and then *"at least this will be my chance to find out if I am what I think I am or if I just hope; if I am going to do what I have taught myself is right or if I am just going to wish I were."*

The story is divided into four parts: (1) the announcement of the death of Colonel Sartoris in Bayard's room, where he is living while attending the university, (2) a flashback to four years earlier, when the Colonel was involved in building the railroad, (3) Bayard's arrival home after his father's death and his confrontation with Drusilla, and (4) Bayard's confrontation with his father's murderer.

The title of the story is significant: for Drusilla, verbena is the only odor that can be smelled above the odor of horses and courage, and it is the flower that Drusilla wears constantly, until she forswears it when she discovers that Bayard is not going to kill Redmond.

When the story begins, some nine years have elapsed. Bayard is now twenty-four years old, and Drusilla and Colonel Sartoris have been married since "the evening when Father and Drusilla had kept old Cash Benbow from becoming United States Marshal and . . . Mrs. Habersham herded them into her carriage and drove them back to town . . . and took Father and Drusilla to the minister herself and saw that they were married." Bayard has been studying law at the university for three years, and he has been living with Professor and Mrs. Wilkins, friends of his late grandmother. The story opens dramatically; Professor Wilkins throws open the door to Bayard's private room and utters, "Bayard. Bayard, my son, my dear son," then says, "Your boy is downstairs in the kitchen." Ringo had summed up what happened in a single, simple statement of fact when he arrived: "They shot Colonel Sartoris this morning. Tell him I be waiting in the kitchen." Bayard is, at first, concerned about horses for the two of them to ride back to Jefferson, but he then realizes that Ringo would naturally have taken care of such matters. He and the Wilkins go the kitchen and find Ringo waiting quietly. Bayard notices that somewhere on the way, Ringo cried; dust is caked in the lines of his face where the tears ran down. As Bayard leaves, Professor Wilkins awkwardly tries to offer Bayard his pistol, but Bayard does not accept it, and this rejection of Professor Wilkins's pistol should prepare us for Bayard's later rejection of Drusilla's pistols. Likewise, Faulkner is very careful here in setting the racial qualities against the older concept of revenge. The word "boy" is still applied to Ringo, even though he is twenty-four, the same age as Bayard, but, by custom, Ringo must wait in the kitchen, an act that suggests the vast social gulf that has come between the two now that they are both men. In the earlier stories, Ringo and Bayard slept together on the same pallet; they were inseparable. Color didn't matter; they joked about Ringo's being "abolished." Now, however, even though Ringo is chronologically a man, he is still a "boy"; Bayard, by contrast, is a young southern gentleman.

On the way back to the Sartoris mansion, Ringo says only one thing to Bayard. He suggests that they could "bushwhack him" (Sartoris' murderer), as they did Grumby. But then he adds: "But I reckon that wouldn't suit that white skin you walks around in." Once again, the difference between the white, twenty-four-year-old Bayard and the black, twenty-four-year-old Ringo is emphasized. It is also ironic that Ringo desires revenge for Colonel Sartoris; the Colonel, it should be remembered, was the great stalwart of "the old southern order," one who would "keep niggers in their place."

During the forty-mile ride back, Bayard envisions what he will see upon arriving at the Sartoris mansion: Colonel Sartoris will be laid out in sartorial splendor, Drusilla will be there with a sprig of verbena in her hair, and she will be holding, proffering to him, two identical, loaded, dueling pistols. In his mind, he envisions her as a "Greek amphora [a classical two-handled Greek vase] priestess of a succinct and formal violence." Drusilla, then, consistent to her characterization throughout the rest of the novel, still represents an ancient concept as old as the Greek civilization; she embodies the need for formal vengeance, a concept that even Colonel Sartoris, ironically, had only recently begun to oppose.

Section two takes us back four years in time; Colonel Sartoris and a friend of his, Ben Redmond, are building the railroad and are still friends, Bayard tells us. (Being friends with the Colonel is not easy, we learn later.) Aunt Jenny Du Pre (the Colonel's sister) has come to live with them, and it is she who plants the flower garden from which Drusilla gathers her verbena to wear because, to her, "verbena was the only scent you could smell above the smell of horses and courage." In the opening of this second section, then, Faulkner emphasizes two important points of this last story in the novel: first, Colonel Sartoris was not an easy person to get along with; it was "easily a record for father" that he and Ben Redmond had been friends for four years. Second, Drusilla is associated with the odor of verbena—the only odor, she believes, which can be smelled above horses and courage. In an earlier story, "Raid," we saw Drusilla's total love for her horse Bobolink; later, we learned about her fighting on horseback against the Yankees, an act some would consider unusually courageous for a woman. Thus, her verbena represents courage—but in terms of violence and bloodshed. Ultimately, even though she totally disapproves of Bayard's refusal to kill Ben Redmond, she does leave him a sprig of verbena, symbolizing the courage which Bayard demonstrates when he confronts Redmond. Bayard's action does encompass a kind of courage for Drusilla, but it is a courage that she cannot accept or fully understand; it forces her to leave the Sartoris home, but not before leaving behind a sprig of verbena, with the intent of never seeing Bayard again.

At the University of Virginia, where Faulkner answered questions about his work, he was asked, "Why is that sprig of verbena left on Bayard's pillow right at the very end?" He responded:

That—of course, the verbena was associated with Drusilla, with that woman, and she had wanted him to take a pistol and avenge his father's death. He went to the man who had shot his father, unarmed, and instead of killing the man, by that gesture he drove the man out of town, and although that had violated Drusilla's traditions of an eye for an eye, she—the sprig of verbena meant that she realized that that took courage too and maybe more moral courage than to have drawn blood, or to have taken another step in a endless feud of an eye for an eye.

When he was asked why Drusilla then left the Sartoris home, Faulkner responded that Drusilla thought that even though it "was a brave thing . . . that sort of bravery is not for me."

Section two also informs and reminds the reader that shortly after the second battle of Manassas, a man named Sutpen was elected as colonel of the regiment that Colonel Sartoris had mustered. This fact further emphasizes that Colonel Sartoris is not an easy person to get along with. Furthermore, we also learn that Colonel Sartoris once killed "a hill man who had been in the first infantry regiment when it voted Father out of command." We are not told what provoked this act or how the Colonel was exonerated of it, nor whether the grudge was against the hill man for voting him out or not. Bayard believes that his father did not hold a grudge against the regiment, but only against Colonel Sutpen, the man who replaced him. (Faulkner's novel *Absalom, Absalom!* recounts the entire story since Colonel Sutpen is the main character of that novel; as noted in the section on Yoknapatawpha County, this type of device by Faulkner unifies the entire imaginative design of his mythical county. In fact, a large portion of these stories was written at the same time that he was writing *Absalom, Absalom!* and published separately.)

Just as Colonel Sartoris was about to forgive Sutpen long enough to ask him to join the "night riders" (a euphemism for the Ku Klux Klan), Sutpen refused and said, "If every man of you would rehabilitate his own land, the country will take care of itself." After that statement, Colonel Sartoris challenged Sutpen to a duel, and Sutpen simply ignored him and walked away, an act which infuriated Colonel Sartoris.

From all this, then, we realize that Colonel Sartoris, while a hero to many people, is, in fact, a hot-headed, impetuous bigot. Even his son Bayard rejects most of his father's values. When Drusilla insists that Colonel Sartoris is working for the entire county, "trying to raise it by its bootstraps," Bayard cannot understand how his father can hold such ideas for the betterment of the country when he is guilty, at the same time, of "killing some of them." When Drusilla maintains that they were just "carpetbaggers," "Northerners," and "foreigners," Bayard can only retaliate by maintaining that the murdered men "were men. Human beings." Drusilla cannot fathom Bayard's humanitarianism. She maintains that there are only a few "dreams in the world," but there are "lots of human lives"; Bayard, in turn, cannot accept the concept that any dream could possibly be worth sacrificing human lives for. Later, Drusilla maintains that "there are worse things than killing men." In retrospect, ever since we first met Drusilla, there has been a strong aura of romantic fatalism, combined with an ancient concept of the godliness of vengeance associated with her.

Bayard then recalls last summer when his father ran against Ben Redmond for the state legislature. Redmond was Colonel Sartoris's partner in the building of the railroad, but the partnership had long since been dissolved. In fact, Bayard wonders how Redmond or anyone could tolerate "Father's violent and ruthless dictatorialness and will to dominate." Significantly, Redmond did not fight during the Civil War; instead, he held a government job, and Colonel Sartoris, who knew that Redmond was honest and courageous, would never let Redmond forget that he was not a soldier; he always found some excuse to taunt Redmond about never "having smelled powder." Finally, they did dissolve their partnership, and Colonel Sartoris bought out Redmond for such a ridiculously low price that they both continued to hate each other. And even after the success of the railroad, Colonel Sartoris was not satisfied; he continued to make absolutely needless allusions to and about Redmond. It finally became so serious that George Wyatt (one of the men who was in the Colonel's troop of irregulars) asked Bayard to try and talk to the Colonel, but Bayard never found an opportunity to do so. Later, when there was an election for the state legislature, Colonel Sartoris defeated Redmond so badly in the election that everyone thought that Colonel Sartoris would now leave Redmond alone, but such was not the case. The Colonel continued to taunt Redmond.

Then last summer, just before Bayard returned to the university for his last year, Drusilla suddenly and unexpectedly told Bayard to kiss her. Bayard responded, "No. You are Father's wife." She insisted, however, and Bayard yielded, and afterward both agreed that he would have to tell his father what happened. That night, Bayard went to his father's office to tell him. Colonel Sartoris was still bemused by the overwhelming win in his favor in the race for state legislature, and when Bayard tells him what happened, Bayard realizes that his father not only did not hear what he said—

he didn't even care if Bayard kissed Drusilla. Instead, he told Bayard how, in the past, he "acted as the land and the time demanded." Now, however, times are changing and Bayard needs to be "trained in the law [so he] can hold [his] own." The Colonel now feels that it is necessary to "do a little moral housecleaning. I am tired of killing men, no matter what the necessity nor the end. Tomorrow, when I go to town and meet Ben Redmond, I shall be unarmed."

The Colonel's entire speech is filled with many ambiguous statements. Faulkner seems to indicate that John Sartoris has no intentions of relinquishing the past or accepting a new order; rather, Colonel Sartoris has only decided to abandon violence and develop more acceptable, effective measures to appease the law while maintaining the southern privileges to which he is accustomed. Colonel Sartoris never concedes defeat; he merely concedes the need for a new strategy to preserve, among other things, racial inequality.

Thus, with this view and with the fact that the Colonel has decided to train Bayard in law, we are further prepared for the fact that Bayard will decide *not* to "take the law into his own hands." The time has now come for a man to put aside personal vengeance and to yield to the orderly process of law and justice.

As is often typical of Faulkner, we are never told why the Colonel *has* to go to meet Redmond. We are never told what finally provoked Redmond to kill Colonel Sartoris. As is also typical of Faulkner, he is more concerned with the causes leading up to the act of violence than he is with the actual violence itself and, afterward, with the results which those acts of violence have on other human beings. In other words, Faulkner is more interested in the psychological states of mind of the people who react to the acts of violence, which will be the central concern of section three.

In section three, there are multiple reactions to Redmond's act of violence: (1) The most powerful, of course, is Drusilla's; she wants vengeance elevated to a sense of nobility. (2) The Colonel's troops expect simple revenge. (3) Aunt Jenny would not care if Bayard spent the day doing nothing—even hiding in the barn loft if he wants to. (4) Ringo expects Redmond to be bushwhacked but knows he can't participate. (5) Redmond is apparently determined to meet Bayard, but not harm him. Finally (6), Bayard must confront Redmond unarmed, if he is to act according to his own code of honor.

In section three, we return to the present moment of the story. Bayard arrives back at the Sartoris mansion and sees not only George Wyatt, but most of Colonel Sartoris's old troop of irregulars all standing at the front of the house "with that curious vulture-like formality which Southern men assume in such situations." Faulkner's evaluations of these men in terms of vultures indicates that Bayard knows that every man there will expect him to take vengeance on his father's murderer. Yet, none of them know that Colonel Sartoris himself has rejected violence and, furthermore, that he conveyed this concept to Bayard—that the time for violence is over, and things must be settled in a peaceful manner. Again, Faulkner inserts the concept that he who lives by the sword shall die by the sword.

Bayard dismisses the men, assuring them that he can handle the situation. He then greets Drusilla and his Aunt Jenny and, after a pause, he goes to his father's coffin and notes that the only thing missing is the intolerance in his father's eyes. It is at this moment, while Bayard is standing by his father's coffin, that Drusilla brings him the two loaded dueling pistols with "the long true barrels true as justice." She then raises her arms and removes two verbena twigs from her hair; one is for his lapel, the other she crushes and drops, for now she abjures verbena forever more. In language, terms, and imagery reminiscent of an ancient Greek tragedy, she stands before Bayard like a Greek goddess of Ancient Revenge and Vengeance. She even elevates the concept of vengeance to a sacred status reserved only for the select few: "How beautiful you are: do you know it? How beautiful: young, to be permitted to kill, to be permitted vengeance, to take into your bare hands the fire of heaven that cast down Lucifer." (Remember that as a woman, she is denied this right.) She then bends down in an attitude of fierce, exultant humility and worshipfully kisses the hand that is going to execute the vengeance. Then, as though a thunderbolt from Jupiter or Jove struck her, she realizes "the bitter and passionate betrayal"—that she has just kissed the hand of a person who does *not* intend to take vengeance. She becomes hysterical, screaming, "I kissed his hand" and then "in an aghast whisper: '*I kissed his hand!*' beginning to laugh, the laughter rising, becoming a scream yet still remaining laughter." Her hysteria mounts until Aunt Jenny asks Louvinia to take her upstairs.

In contrast to Drusilla and the "vulture-like men," Aunt Jenny hopes that Bayard will not feel the need for revenge. Her eyes are just like the Colonel's eyes, Faulkner tells us, except that Aunt Jenny's eyes are lacking in intolerance; she is a wise and tolerant lady and she has seen enough of revenge and bloodshed. She prefers that Bayard reject such primitive ideas. Other people's concepts of bravery and cowardice mean nothing to her.

In section four, Bayard awakens to the odor of verbena ("the only scent you could smell above the smell of horses and courage"), and thus this section renews the question of courage: what constitutes an act of courage? When Bayard prepares to go to town to confront his father's murderer, Aunt Jenny tells him that if he wants to stay hidden in the stable loft all day, she will still respect him; her eyes show that she is wise and tolerant. Before leaving, Bayard mounts the stairs to Drusilla's room, but again she merely bursts out in hysterical laughter, repeating, "*I kissed his hand.*"

As Bayard rides into town, Ringo catches up with him and when they arrive in town, Ringo wants to go in with Bayard to confront Ben Redmond, but Bayard will not permit it. As noted previously, in terms of "the old order" of the South, no Negro could possibly be permitted to participate in an act of revenge against a white person. And it is ironic that Ringo desires a revenge that Bayard, the son, does not; the irony, of course, is that the Colonel would not recognize Ringo or any Negro as being a proper person to revenge his death.

When Bayard meets George Wyatt and "five or six others of father's old troop," they all automatically assume that Bayard, who at age fifteen revenged his grandmother's murder, will naturally revenge his own father's murder. George Wyatt even tries to force a pistol onto Bayard. Then in a moment of silent communication, something is sensed—unspoken—between Bayard and George Wyatt; Wyatt, like Drusilla, knows that Bayard is *not* going to shed blood. Bayard is going to confront his father's murderer unarmed. Wyatt doesn't understand since he knows that Bayard is no coward; he simply reminds Bayard that Ben Redmond is also a brave man.

When Bayard enters Redmond's office, he notes a pistol lying in front of Redmond on the top of his desk. Bayard watches as Redmond lifts the pistol to fire it, and he realizes that it is not aimed at him. Yet he stands there as Redmond fires twice and then walks out of the office, passes between George Wyatt and the throng of men gathered outside, and goes to the train station. He "went away from Jefferson and from Mississippi and never came back." When one considers courage, Redmond's actions here cannot be ignored; it would indeed take a brave man to walk through the crowd of Sartoris family friends, with all of them assuming that he had just killed Bayard Sartoris.

The men then rush into Redmond's office, and when they realize what has happened, they don't fully understand, but they tremendously admire the courage that it took for Bayard to act as he did—to face Redmond unarmed—and they admit that "maybe there has been enough killing" in the Sartoris family. This idea echoes and affirms Colonel Sartoris's concepts expressed at the end of section two of this story.

Bayard and Ringo go back to the Sartoris plantation, and Bayard sleeps out in the pasture for five hours. When he arrives back at the manor house, Aunt Jenny tells him that Drusilla left on the afternoon train. Bayard goes to his room, and there he sees a single sprig of verbena lying on his pillow.

It is possible to say that Bayard did not avenge his father's death because he knew that his father had been a ruthless and power-hungry man, a murderer of innocent people, and a dominating, intolerant and dictatorial man. These statements are all true, and we know from Bayard's comments that he knows all of his father's faults, but from the first story in this novel, "Ambuscade," where there was an unabashed adoration for his father, to the moment when Bayard approaches his father's coffin with his breath panting, we know that there is a deep love between Bayard and his father—despite all of the Colonel's faults. One could also maintain that Bayard knows that Colonel Sartoris, in his obsession with power, pushed Redmond beyond all bounds of endurance and that, ultimately, any man as threatened as Redmond was with humiliation, would eventually strike back. This, too, might contribute to Bayard's decision not to avenge his father's death, but there is one more, far more important reason why Bayard does not kill Redmond.

Bayard's ultimate manhood is seen in his refusal to kill Ben Redmond. Most men of that time would have easily yielded to the pressures of the community. Bayard even tells Aunt Jenny that he wants "to be well thought of." And according to the code of that time, a son should avenge his father's murder. Ultimately, Bayard does not reject the code; instead, he rises above that code and follows the course of law and order that he has been studying for over three years at the university. In addition, Bayard is also following another code: "Thou shalt not kill." To follow this higher code means that Bayard placed his own life in serious danger: he knew that he had to go and see Redmond; he had to at least confront Redmond. Otherwise he could not have lived either with himself or within the community: "maybe forever after could never again hold up" his head.

In conclusion, even though others, especially Drusilla because of her ancient code of blood vengeance, cannot understand Bayard's actions, in the final analysis, even she acknowledges that Bayard's actions are not those of a coward: it takes a far braver person—unarmed—to confront an enemy than it does to kill someone in cold blood. Finally, after a bloody Civil War and a horrifying Reconstruction, Bayard's actions suggest that the South will enter into an era of law and order.

CHARACTER ANALYSES

Bayard Sartoris

In many ways, *The Unvanquished* can be seen as a *Bildungsroman*—that is, as a novel tracing the growth of a character from youth to manhood. The seven stories in this volume cover Bayard's growing up—from the time he is twelve years old in "Ambuscade" until he is twenty-four years old in "An Odor of Verbena." At twelve, he is on the verge of manhood, but he is still playing childish games of war; at twenty-four, he is in full possession of his mature powers and asserts them in "An Odor of Verbena," finally putting an end to unnecessary violence. Each story, however, since it was published separately, is able to stand alone, without relying too heavily on the other stories; consequently, even though we see Bayard changing and maturing in one story, sometimes that change occurs only within the context of that certain story and does not carry over from one story to the next. Of the seven stories, we see a Bayard who does not change too much in the first three stories; then we view a Bayard who undergoes a tremendous change in the fourth and fifth stories. Finally, Faulkner presents a mature and distinguished Bayard Sartoris in the last story.

The early stories, particularly "Ambuscade," show Bayard as a young boy who looks upon war as a type of game to be played, a game with no serious consequences. The Civil War is far away, somewhere in the distance. The towns that are talked about are all outside the geographical region of Jefferson and Yoknapatawpha County. Therefore, Bayard and Ringo create imaginary war games, using sand as forts and fortifications—insubstantial fortifications which Loosh can, and does, easily destroy. The ease, in fact, with which these fortifications are destroyed seems to suggest the immaturity of the young boys who are constructing them.

The "pot shot" which Bayard takes at one of the Yankees is only a juvenile extension of the war games which he and Ringo are playing. Bayard does not realize the full seriousness of taking a shot at a Yankee. His immaturity is further seen in the final scene of this story; he is so young and so physically small that both he and Ringo are able to hide underneath Granny's hoop skirts while the Yankee soldiers are searching for them elsewhere. Also in this first story of the novel, Bayard accepts Ringo, his little Negro friend, as either an equal or as someone superior in knowledge to himself. As in other of Faulkner's works, young children often do not have the racial prejudices of adult society. Thus, for some time to come, Bayard continues to accept Ringo as an equal, but at the end of the novel, in "An Odor of Verbena," when we see Bayard's final maturation, he and Ringo are presented as two adults—one white male and one black male—and both are keenly aware of the racial difference between them.

Throughout the episodes with the "mule trading" or "borrowing," Bayard is constantly seen assuming more and more responsibility; at the same time, he begins to do fewer childish pranks. But in all of these early stories, the greatest change within Bayard takes place when Granny is murdered by Grumby. According to the southern code of honor, no gentleman would ever harm a woman or child; this dictum is first and foremost. This same code demands that if a woman is killed by a man, then one of that woman's male relatives must avenge her death. Bayard's father is off with his troop of irregulars; no one knows where he is. Thus, the task falls to Bayard. Bayard, in assuming the responsibility for avenging Granny's murder, assumes a role that calls for strong maturity and courage. Bayard, at fifteen, is forced by the southern code of his society to assume a role that many grown men would find difficult or impossible to perform.

The manner, the diligence, and the determination that Bayard exhibits in tracking down Grumby are such that Bayard wins our complete approval and admiration, in addition to that of the entire adult population of Jefferson, for Bayard performs an act that is distinctively more than courageous. His ultimate slaying of Grumby proves that he is a true Sartoris, upholding "the old order" of the South. After all, Granny always divided the profits of her schemes among the entire population of the county, and everyone was obligated to her. They loved her and they depended on her. It is not surprising that after Bayard successfully avenges her murder, he not only would win the approbation of the county's population, but that he would also add to the grand, almost mystical, aura surrounding the Sartoris name.

Bayard's continued maturation occurs during his conversation with his father when he learns that the Colonel is tired of killing people; the war is over and too many people have been killed. It is now a time for a restoration of law and order. This conversation, plus Bayard's studying law at the university, are some of the factors which influence his final actions in the story, "An Odor of Verbena." Since Bayard captured the imagination of the entire county by his pursuit of Grumby, it was tacitly assumed that he would, unquestionably, avenge the death of his own father, Colonel Sartoris, the stalwart of the county. After all, nine years ago, Bayard performed an act of such bravery that no one questions what he will do now. Thus when Bayard confronts Redmond unarmed and is responsible for Redmond's leaving town, no one in Jefferson questions Bayard's courage or his manner of handling the situation. Everyone realizes that it takes more courage to confront a man unarmed, as Bayard does, than it does to kill a man. This is the most influential lesson that Bayard learns from his father. At the novel's end, Bayard has developed from a young child playing games of war into a youth capable of tracking down a murderer and has finally become a young gentleman of law who bravely rejects an act of violence and endorses a code of law and order.

Colonel John Sartoris

Colonel Sartoris is Faulkner's most enigmatic character. He is the most admired man in Yoknapatawpha County and, at the same time, he is probably one of the most difficult people to get along with in the entire county. Bayard makes a telling statement about his father in "Ambuscade." "He was not big," Bayard realizes, "it was just the things he did, that we knew he was doing, had been doing in Virginia and Tennessee, that made him seem big to us." In fact, when Colonel Sartoris ascends the stairs at home, his long sword often strikes against the steps but, mounted upon his large horse Jupiter (an apt name for his horse since Jupiter was the supreme deity of the ancient Roman gods), the Colonel seems to loom over everyone else.

At the beginning of the war, Colonel Sartoris is the first man to raise a regiment to fight against the Yankees. But, as we later discover, within one year the Colonel was voted out of his command and another man was voted in as Colonel of the regiment. Colonel Sartoris then left and came back to Yoknapatawpha County to organize his own troop of irregulars. We do not know exactly why he was voted out, but all indications point to his arrogance—his insistence that "right or wrong, John Sartoris is right," according to one of his loyal men (George Wyatt). Colonel Sartoris cannot be second in command; he is unable to take orders from anyone else. Thus, he literally deserts the Confederate Army and raises a troop of irregulars under the command of no one except himself; he is responsible to no one but himself. This is why he is considered a renegade by the Yankee forces and why they have issued a reward for his capture. In modern times, Sartoris's actions and tactics would be similar to guerrilla warfare, which was, in those times, completely unacceptable; during the Civil War, it was expected that great armies should confront each other directly. However, as the leader of a troop of irregulars, Colonel Sartoris becomes somewhat of an instant legend; he seems to be always in the vicinity or in the neighboring land, protecting women and children who have been left defenseless while their menfolk are off fighting in Virginia for some general whose name no one is familiar with. Everyone knows about Sartoris though; everyone hears about his feats and, consequently, he becomes the hometown folk hero; either he personally has protected many of the local families or else he has helped protect their kinfolks. However, we, the readers, *must* keep in mind that if this folk hero, Colonel Sartoris, had not been voted out of his command, he too would have been away in Virginia and not in home territory, "protecting" the women and children.

We do, however, admire his cleverness. When Colonel Sartoris is able to surround about sixty Yankee soldiers, capture them by a clever ruse with only a few men, make the Yankees think that they are surrounded by a large Confederate force, and make them shed their guns and clothes—these actions in "Retreat" show Sartoris to be a man of great resourcefulness, military intelligence, and dashing bravery. We also admire his cleverness in the many ways that he is able to elude the enemy. For example, the way he pretends to be old, infirm, and "born looney" to escape from the Yankee patrol, again in "Retreat," is yet another aspect of his cleverness.

Colonel Sartoris is also a man who is supremely self-assured. He exudes confidence in everything he does. The absolute and undeviating loyalty he inspires in the men he commands attests to his ability to lead with authority and respect. The fact that earlier his arrogance caused him to be demoted in his official capacity does not detract from the fact that as a commander of his own troop of irregulars, he receives extraordinary loyalty and devotion from his fellow rebels.

He is also able to inspire confidence in men in matters other than war-time tactics. At the end of the war, Sartoris is broke and destitute, yet he has a dream of building a railroad, and he is apparently able to communicate that dream to others and to convince enough of them to finance him in his dream—not just once, but over and over again—so that the railroad is built and even the first engine is bought and financed. Sartoris had no money; he had only a vision and courage and the determination to be, as Faulkner's title states, unvanquished.

Colonel Sartoris, however, is also a man of intolerance and violence; he has a short temper and, during the war, he became accustomed to killing people who disagreed with him. We hear that he killed (the reason is never given) a "hill man" who was in his first command. As compensation, he sent the man's widow some money; interestingly, she was neither appeased nor afraid of him; she came down from the hills, flung the money in his face, spat, and left. After the war is over, to prevent blacks from voting, Sartoris kills two Missouri carpetbaggers, one an old man and the other a very young boy. Even though either the old man or the young boy shot first, we question the extreme measure of killing in order to prevent the voting. Surely, Colonel Sartoris and his troop of men, who were gathered outside the Holston Hotel (the voting place), could have removed the old man and the boy without killing them.

Of course, however, Colonel Sartoris commits the murders for reasons which he considers valid. Two outsiders, two foreigners, had crossed several states, had come South, and had invaded his county for one reason: to force upon the native population laws and customs which are alien to the territory. To Sartoris, the Missouri (originally New England) carpetbaggers are intruders; they have no right to use the desolation of the land to try and alter so suddenly and so completely the social customs and traditions of the region. Seen in this context, the actions of the Colonel are justified; to his fellow southern whites, he is merely defending the rights and traditions of their region against unwarranted outside interference.

To his son Bayard, Colonel Sartoris's major flaw is his intolerance. When Bayard looks at his father's corpse laid out in the coffin, the main difference that he notes is that the "intolerance in his [closed] eyes" is missing. The other difference is the Colonel's hands; the hands which had performed so many acts of violence are now lying clumsy, still, and inert. In contrast is the Colonel's sister; Faulkner emphasizes that the Colonel's sister has eyes that are wise and tolerant. Remember that it was partly because of the Colonel's intolerance that he was voted out of his first regiment. Likewise, his intolerance does not allow an opinion different from his. Bayard, George Wyatt (the Colonel's most fervent admirer), and others feel that he needles his partner, Ben Redmond, far beyond the bounds of endurance. They are amazed that Redmond is able to tolerate the Colonel's insults for as long as he does. Colonel Sartoris had no intention of running for the legislature until he found out that Ben Redmond was going to run as a candidate. Then he also decided to run—simply to spite Redmond. Since Colonel Sartoris was such a popular and well known local hero, he naturally won the election by an overwhelming majority.

In spite of all his flaws, which are numerous, Colonel Sartoris finally realizes, near the end of the novel, that he has killed enough men: "Tomorrow, when I meet Ben Redmond, I shall be unarmed," he says in "An Odor of Verbena." He feels that in the past he acted as the times demanded, but now he realizes that the times have changed: the war is over; it is now a time for law and order. In fact, if the promised federal troops had arrived, it would not have been necessary for him to confront the carpet-baggers and kill them, but since they failed to arrive as promised, he felt that the times demanded that he take matters into his own hands.

Faulkner seems also to indicate that John Sartoris has no intentions of relinquishing the past or accepting a new order; rather, Colonel Sartoris has only decided to abandon *violence* and develop more acceptable, effective measures to appease the law while maintaining the southern privileges to which he is accustomed. Colonel Sartoris never concedes defeat; he merely concedes the need for a new strategy to preserve, among other things, racial inequality.

Furthermore, he sends his only son to the university to study law because now is the time to restore law and order to the land. Thus, in the final analysis, even though the Colonel is filled with pride, arrogance, intolerance, and an obsession with power, he represents the best of the South. John Sartoris is the stalwart of the South, possessed with virtue, nobility, valor, and a deeply embedded loyal devotion to the customs of the southern culture and a deep desire to retain those long-honored traditions.

Granny (Miss Rosa Millard)

Because we first see Granny through the eyes of her twelve-year-old grandson, it is easy to be misled in our opinion of her. Too many critics have simply dismissed her as a romanticized, stereotyped, indomitable southern matriarch who accomplishes feats far beyond the capacity of a woman of her age and physical stature. For both Bayard and Ringo, she truly does seem to loom larger than life, but then we must remember that when Bayard sees her lying dead, murdered by Grumby, she looks "like she had been made out of a lot of little thin dry light sticks, notched together and braced with cord, and now the cord had broken and all the little sticks had collapsed in a quiet heap on the floor."

Granny assumes that all people, certainly southerners, possess the same values, ethics, and manners as she herself possesses. She belongs to that old southern tradition that holds tradition itself as the standard for right or wrong. She assumes that an army officer will be a gentleman—even a Yankee officer; therefore, when she lies about the whereabouts of the two boys in "Ambuscade," she does so with the full knowledge and belief that no gentleman would ever question the veracity of a lady. The irony, of course, is that this belief allows the southern lady to lie prodigiously because a true southern gentleman would never confront her or accuse her of lying—much less call her an outright liar. (As a sidenote, Faulkner wrote stories such as "Dry September" in which a black man is violently killed because a southern lady lies about his raping her; because of the southern code, white southern men would naturally kill a "nigger" before they would question the veracity of a white lady.)

Granny is obviously a product of "the old order" of the South. She would never consider adapting, inwardly or outwardly, to a South other than the one in which she was reared. She cannot understand the concept of a Negro desiring anything other than serving his white master. In "Raid," she often tells the Negroes to "go back home"—meaning, of course, to return to their white masters' plantations and to their positions as slaves, serving obediently their white masters. Granny's loyalty to the "holy cause" of the Confederacy, which God has "seen fit to make . . . a lost cause" permits her to indulge in a morality replete with contradictions. As a result of her own individual sense of morality, Granny will steal horses, but will not let Ringo and Bayard ride them in to town to do an errand for her at Mrs. Compson's. To Granny, the horses are not stolen; they are "borrowed." She will involve young Bayard and Ringo in forgery and theft; yet, at the same time, she will force the boys to kneel down and pray for forgiveness for having "lied."

In yet another ritual of penitence, Granny rationalizes her wrongful actions in one of the most unusual prayers ever uttered—a prayer that is admirable because there is no cringing; yet neither is there awe, reverence, or humility. Granny's prayer to God is almost a challenge or a defiance to God. Yet in her prayer, she is noble in that she wants all of God's punishment for the "sins" committed to fall on her shoulders: no one else is to be blamed. Her prayer to God is direct and matter-of-fact: "I did not sin for revenge [even though at this point, she has cause for revenge since she can see no reason for the Yankees' burning of the Sartoris mansion]. I defy You or anyone to say I did. I sinned first for justice. And after that first time . . . I sinned for the sake of food and clothes for your own creatures." Then she *informs* God that if she "kept some of it back . . . *I am the best judge of that* (emphasis mine). Granny, therefore, is truly admirable in her concern for other people, for her courage, for her direct honesty with God and people, and for her willingness to assume full responsibility for her acts. Yet despite her genuine humanitarian concerns, Granny never is able to accept or understand a code of morality which would enable her to put an individual above the traditional southern codes and customs of "the old order." She refuses to consider Negroes as being anything other than possessions of their white masters. Oblivious of their human rights, she tries to coerce the recently freed, disoriented Negroes following their Yankee liberators into returning to Alabama and to their proper position as slaves by rewarding them with food and protection. However, as good as her intentions are, Miss Rosa Millard is a victim of her heritage ("the old order"); she is at the same time both noble and immoral, a combination of contradictions of which she is totally unaware. For example, Ringo is good enough to be Granny's partner and "equal" in her dealings with Ab Snopes and with the Yankees, and he can sit with her on the front seat of her wagon, yet in church, where all God's people should be equal, Ringo must sit apart from the whites (up in the gallery, with the other Negroes); it is only later, when Granny begins apportioning money and mules to the poor that Ringo is allowed to leave the gallery and read the names from Granny's big account book. He is allowed to leave the gallery, but his position is still that of a subservient black. Granny's motivations are sincerely altruistic, but her manner is unconsciously that of *La Grande Dame*, doling out alms to the poor.

In conclusion, Granny is one of the best examples of "the old order" of the South. When she realizes that the southern cause is lost and that the Colonel will be returning, she also realizes that she must have some cash to hand over to him so that he can begin again. Thus Granny engages in one last, fatal confrontation with Grumby. Importantly, she will not let Ringo and Bayard accompany her; she thinks that they look old enough for Grumby to consider them dangerous; but she mistakenly assumes that because Grumby is a southerner, he is by definition also a gentleman and, consequently, he would never "hurt a woman. Even Yankees do not harm old women." Granny goes to her death as one of the unvanquished because of her tenacious belief in the ideals of "the old order."

Granny is, in one sense, a great humanitarian, but she is at the same time totally incapable of understanding the causes which motivated the Civil War itself; she cannot understand the need of a human being to desire his freedom; she cannot understand the need of a human being to feel pride in his own humanity even though his skin is black; and therefore she contents herself, instead, with helping the individual, unfortunate human beings she encounters— black or white—to survive in a time of destruction and chaos.

Drusilla Hawk Sartoris

In some ways, Drusilla Hawk is one of Faulkner's strongest and most determined defenders of "the old order" of the South. In other ways, she is the greatest violator of "the old order." We first hear of Drusilla when her brother tells Bayard and Ringo how she defied the Yankees who were about to take her horse. She threatens to kill her horse (a horse she is deeply fond of) rather than let the Yankees take it. This extraordinary act of daring (and sacrifice, if necessary) characterizes Drusilla as being different from all the other women in the novel.

When Drusilla's fiancé, Gavin Breckbridge, is killed at the Battle of Shiloh and, later, when Drusilla's father is killed in the war, Drusilla shows no grief in the traditional southern manner of copious weeping and wearing black; her mother, Louisa, thinks that Drusilla has deliberately tried to "unsex herself" because of her refusal to weep. For Drusilla, however, weeping would accomplish nothing, whereas riding out to the front lines and killing Yankees would be an act that would avenge the deaths of her loved ones. Ultimately, Drusilla becomes, in Faulkner's words, the representative of "the Greek amphora priestess of a succinct and formal violence." Consistent with Faulkner's characterization from her first act of defending her horse to her final act of laying a sprig of verbena on Bayard's pillow before she leaves the Sartoris manor forever, Drusilla represents an ancient concept as old as the Greek civilization—that is, the *need* for formal vengeance: Drusilla is like the Greek Electra who, when her father was killed by his wife, demanded her own mother's death as an act of formal revenge.

When Drusilla says that she wants to ride with Colonel Sartoris's troops, the idea is so foreign and so bizarre that Bayard never even mentions it to his father. Yet Drusilla is serious; she feels that she must kill Yankees to avenge the deaths of both her father and her fiancé. The fact that women have seldom fought in wars never occurs to her; yet what she does is akin to heresy in terms of southern tradition. For Drusilla to dress as a common soldier and sleep on the ground in the same bivouac area and fight and kill Yankees—as a man would—gives credence to her mother's accusation that Drusilla has "unsexed herself." That Drusilla has courage, daring, decisiveness, and resourcefulness is never questioned; but all the qualities which are commonly associated with being a woman are burned out of her by her experiences (not just the deaths) during the war and its aftermath. A major change occurs within the woman: when we first meet Drusilla, in "Retreat," even though her hands are "hard and scratched like a man's," she is sensitive and filled with compassion about the plight of the Negroes. Several times, she has gone to the river where swarms of newly freed, confused, and bewildered Negroes are trying to cross over "the river Jordan" and get to "the Promised Land." The Yankees are readying to blow up the bridge, but Drusilla's mother, Louisa, is unmoved. She says, simply, "We cannot be responsible. The Yankees brought it on themselves: let them pay the price." Drusilla answers, "Those Negroes are not Yankees"; like Granny, who is a representative of "the old order," Drusilla has a true humanitarian concern for the plight of the Negroes, but at the same time, she will see to it, as she does in "Skirmish at Sartoris," that the Negro remain in his or her assigned place—that is, as an inferior to the whites. She is fiercely loyal to John Sartoris in his attempt to keep the blacks from voting.

The war denies Drusilla the opportunity to function as an antebellum southern lady; she has lost two men she loves deeply and the South's principles and social convictions have been challenged. The idea of staying behind, trying to hold together the remnants of family life, is impossible for her. She chooses a man's role, and her success in "unsexing herself" (Louisa's term) is most clearly evident when the older women of the community insist on treating Drusilla *not* as a returning soldier and fighter, but as a woman who has compromised herself. When she cries out, "We went to the war to hurt Yankees, not hunting women," she unconsciously reveals how thoroughly she has aligned herself with the thinking of the men she fought alongside of. Her mother is right; to a degree, Drusilla does "unsex herself." But the women ultimately defeat her when they make her put on a dress. Once more, she has to assume the appearance of a lady. But not before she participates in one last act of violence to preserve the code of "the old order." Drusilla is the only other person in the room when Colonel Sartoris kills the carpetbaggers, and Faulkner indicates that Drusilla is thrilled by these murders; John Sartoris is upholding the principles of "the old order," and this, to Drusilla, is far more important than the marriage ceremony which she forgot all about, even though that was the reason she came to town and even though she took part in the skirmish in full bridal attire.

While there is no mention of any love between Drusilla and Colonel Sartoris, it is clear that Drusilla embraces John's dreams and hopes and believes that they are worth all the killing and pain that happens because of them. Drusilla argues with Bayard that Colonel Sartoris is "thinking of the whole country which he is trying to raise by its bootstraps." She accepts as normal the fact that some people must get killed in the process. In terms of traditional roles, a woman is the nurturer of life, not its destroyer. But Drusilla believes that "there are not many dreams in the world, but there are a lot of human lives. And one human life or two dozen—."

It is not surprising, therefore, that after her husband is killed, that she expects his son to become his avenger and his successor. The scene is archetypal: Bayard, the son, is standing by his father's coffin when Drusilla, dressed in a yellow ball gown, with sprigs of verbena in her hair, her eyes shining with fierce exultation and her voice "silvery and triumphant," extends to him the two loaded duelling pistols with "the long true barrels true as justice." Here she is the figure of Woman as Avenger, as was the Greek Electra. She stands before Bayard fully expecting him to perform the full measure of revenge and vengeance, and here she even elevates the concept of revenge to a sacred status reserved only for the select few, of whom Bayard is one of the fortunate ones.

When Drusilla realizes that he is not going to carry out the act of revenge, she becomes hysterical. However, the next day when

Bayard returns, he finds that Drusilla has gone forever, but she left for him a sprig of verbena—that symbol of courage which she has always worn. Thus, even though Drusilla can respect Bayard's courage, she cannot change what she has become and, as a result, she must depart forever from Bayard's life.

Ringo

In the first story, "Ambuscade," Ringo is the black playmate and the constant companion of Bayard Sartoris, a young white adolescent; both are twelve years old. The South has been at war for two years, and Ringo belongs to the race of people about whom the war is being fought. Neither Bayard nor Ringo is fully aware of this fact, however. War is the subject of stories and games. The bloody front lines and the matter of racial segregation are far away from the world where we first meet Bayard and Ringo as they are "playing war" behind the Sartoris smokehouse.

Ringo enthusiastically joins in the game with Bayard, recreating battles which would, ironically, keep the entire Negro race enslaved; he even likes, and insists on having, a turn playing one of the southern white generals, and Bayard has to play one of the northern ones. Ironically, Ringo is simply too immature to know the social significance of the games; he sees the Yankees as enemies of the Sartoris family and, therefore, as enemies to himself. There seems to be little or no realization on his part that other Negroes are "escaping" to their freedom. The thought of joining the other Negroes never occurs to Ringo.

Ringo has so thoroughly adopted the white values of the Sartoris family that his judgments are exact replicas of the white society of the South. From "Ambuscade"—where both he and Bayard, a black boy and a white boy, hide under Granny's skirts—until "Vendée," where both boys track down Grumby, kill him, and return home and fall asleep exhausted together on a pallet, there is little or no significant difference between them. In fact, Ringo is more often than not in charge of Granny's "mule borrowing" operation and seems more clever at it than Bayard does.

Even at the end of "An Odor of Verbena," Ringo feels that Colonel Sartoris should be revenged. But by now, the color code of southern society has dictated that Ringo, a Negro, can have nothing to do with the Colonel's death being revenged. Ringo's only participation in the matter is his serving as a messenger to Bayard, who must do the avenging. Whereas other whites come to Bayard to offer their services—some even offering to avenge the Colonel's death by killing Redmond themselves—Ringo does not have these options. Were he even to raise his voice to the white man who killed the Colonel, Ringo's life would be endangered. It is further irony that Ringo would even want the Colonel's death revenged because all his life the Colonel fought to keep the Negroes enslaved and, later, he prevented them from exercising their right to vote.

It is not clear when the breech between Bayard and Ringo occurs. Faulkner does not tell us. As was noted, when both were youths Ringo was considered the smarter of the two, but some time between "Vendée" (when both are almost sixteen and more or less equals) and "An Odor of Verbena" (when both are twenty-four), a significant gulf has developed between them. For example, when they were young, they slept together on the same pallet; yet in the last story of the volume, Ringo cannot even enter Bayard's room to announce the Colonel's death; he must announce it to Professor Wilkins and wait in the kitchen until Bayard comes down to him. Ringo is, ultimately, not his own man. He is a person or pawn molded by the values of the old southern society that he grew up in, believed in, and is still ensnared in when the novel ends.

QUESTIONS FOR REVIEW

1. From the first to the final story, trace Bayard's development from a young child, playing war games, to a fully mature man of courage.

2. Discuss Ringo's change in character, as a result of the color of his skin; in the early stories, he assumes a role equal to Bayard, but in the later stories he is denied participation in the actions of the stories.

3. Characterize Granny's religious views.

4. What characteristics does Colonel Sartoris possess that make him so idolized by the people of the county?

5. Who are "the unvanquished" of these stories?

6. What are some of the values attached to "the old order" of the South?

7. Why does Bayard avenge his grandmother's death, but then refuse to avenge his own father's death?

8. What is the relationship between Colonel Sartoris and Drusilla?

9. Characterize Ab Snopes and his relationship to "the old order" of the South.

10. Would you consider this book to be a collection of short stories, dealing with the same characters, or is it more of a novel with a definite structure of its own? Why or why not?

SELECTED BIBLIOGRAPHY

BACKMAN, MELVIN. *Faulkner: The Major Years: A Critical Study.* Bloomington: Indiana University Press, 1966. The chief value of this study is that it gives many of the prominent critical theories about the major novels.

BROOKS, CLEANTH. *William Faulkner: The Yoknapatawpha Novels.* Yale, 1963. One of the outstanding studies on Faulkner, it has a section at the back filled with many individual insights into individual problems.

CAMPBELL, HARRY M., and RUEL E. FOSTER. *William Faulkner.* Norman: University of Oklahoma Press, 1953. One of the earlier studies, it is useful as a basic guide from which other critics evolved their theories.

CULLEN, JOHN B., and FLOYD C. WATKINS. *Old Times in the Faulkner Country.* Chapel Hill: The University of North Carolina Press, 1961.

FAULKNER, WILLIAM. *Faulkner in the University,* ed. FREDERICK L. GWYNN, and JOSEPH L. BLOTNER. Charlottesville: University of

Virginia, 1959. A series of taped questions put to Faulkner by students at the University of Virginia along with Faulkner's answers.

HOFFMAN, FREDERICK, and OLGA VICKERY (eds.). *William Faulkner: Three Decades of Criticism.* East Lansing: Michigan State University Press, 1960. A collection of some of the best essays written on Faulkner. A very valuable reference book.

HOFFMAN, FREDERICK. *William Faulkner.* New York: Twayne Publishers, 1961. A basic introduction to Faulkner as a writer.

HOWE, IRVING. *William Faulkner: A Critical Study.* New York: Random House, 1952. A general interpretation that gives a broad view of Faulkner even though there is a deficiency of "in depth" criticism.

HUNT, JOHN W[ESLEY]. *William Faulkner: Art in Theological Tension.* Syracuse, N.Y.: Syracuse University Press, 1965.

LONGLEY, JOHN LEWIS, JR. *The Tragic Mask: A Study of Faulkner's Heroes.* Chapel Hill: University of North Carolina Press, 1963.

MALIN, IRVING. *William Faulkner, an Interpretation.* Stanford: Stanford University Press, 1957.

MILLGATE, MICHAEL. *William Faulkner.* New York: Grove Press, 1961. A useful introduction, particularly for the beginning student of Faulkner.

MINER, WARD L. *The World of William Faulkner.* New York: Grove Press, 1959. A brief account of Faulkner's family and the Mississippi environment.

O'CONNOR, WILLIAM VAN. *The Tangled Fire of William Faulkner.* Minneapolis: University of Minnesota Press, 1960. Contains many excellent chapters even though some chapters on some novels deal with a rather specific aspect of the novel.

RUNYAN, HARRY A. *A Faulkner Glossary.* New York: Citadel Press, 1964.

SLATOFF, WALTER J. *Quest for Failure: A Study of William Faulkner.* Ithaca, N.Y.: Cornell University Press, 1960.

SWIGGART, PETER. *The Art of Faulkner's Novels.* Austin: University of Texas Press, 1962. One of the best studies of Faulkner's major novels, it discusses the greatness of Faulkner's art.

THOMPSON, LAWRENCE. *William Faulkner: An Introduction and Interpretation.* New York: Barnes and Noble, 1963. Perhaps the best short study yet to appear on Faulkner, this volume brings together many of the obvious critical views about Faulkner.

VICKERY, OLGA W. *The Novels of William Faulkner.* Baton Rouge: Louisiana Press, 1959. Perhaps the finest book yet to appear on Faulkner. Mrs. Vickery handles most of Faulkner's fiction in depth.

WAGGONER, HYATT H. *William Faulkner: From Jefferson to the World.* Lexington: University of Kentucky Press, 1959.

WARREN, ROBERT PENN (ed.). *Faulkner: A Collection of Critical Essays.* Englewood Cliffs, N.J.: Prentice Hall, 1966.

NOTES